The Devil's Dictionary of Education

Tyrrell Burgess

continuum
LONDON • NEW YORK

Continuum
The Tower Building
11 York Road
London SE1 7NX
www.continuumbooks.com

370 Lexington Avenue
New York
NY 10017-6503

First published 2002

British Library Cataloguing-in-Publication Data
A catalogue record for this book is available from the British Library.

ISBN: 0-8264-6323-1 (paperback)

Typeset by C.K.M. Typesetting, Salisbury, Wiltshire
Printed and bound in Great Britain by Biddles Ltd, *www.biddles.co.uk*

Contents

Acknowledgements

As the example of Dr Johnson shows, one cannot attempt a lexicon unless one reads and listens a lot. The unmatchable models for one such as this are of course Ambrose Bierce's *The Devil's Dictionary* and Gustave Flaubert's *Dictionary of Received Ideas*. My view of education has benefited from reading, over many years, the work of Karl Popper and, recently, of Raymond Tallis. People I have particularly listened to include Joan Burgess, Philip Marples, John Pratt and Joanna Swann. Where the source of a definition is known it is referred to in the text. The public authorities in education have been a perpetual source of inspiration and delight. Marc Burgess has made the whole thing feasible by making the computer run like clockwork.

List of Abbreviations

adj.   adjective
adv.   adverb
anon.   author unknown
cf.   compare
COD.   Concise Oxford Dictionary
conj.   conjunction
dub.   dubious
etym.   etymology
f.   from
ger.   gerund
interj.   interjection
n.   noun
n.pl.   plural noun
obs.   obsolete
part.   participle
perh.   perhaps
pr.n.   proper noun
prep.   preposition
pron.   pronoun
q.v.   which (word) see
qq.v.   which (words) see
sc.   to wit
sent. sub.   sentence substitute
suff.   suffix
trad.   traditional
v.   verb
viz.   namely

To the victims of education everywhere

A Learner's Lexicon

A level: *n.*   (i) rite of passage for eighteen-year-olds at school or college

    (ii) a shibboleth on the brink of a university

    (iii) a level

abecedarian: *n.*   (i) tyro or rookie with pretensions to literacy

    (ii) name of a project in North Carolina showing that educational 'intervention' from birth to five years old produced gains in IQ and achievement still visible ten years later, but the intervention was massive and the gains, though welcome, marginal

ability: *n.*   (i) the second of the legal criteria for the suitability of a child's education (the others are age and aptitude, qq.v.): there is no known way of identifying it and no attempt is being made to find one, hence

    (ii) that which is revealed by tests, usually something that those tested cannot do

able: *adj.*   tediously adequate to a task: to be more risks being called brilliant and thus distrusted and reviled

abnormal: *adj.*   different from most: a pejorative expression applied, for example, to the oddly stupid rather than to the oddly clever, who are gifted or exceptional

absenteeism: *n.*   truancy among teachers

academic: *adj.*   (i) scholarly or precise
(ii) of no use, interest or consequence

academic dress: *n.*   mediaevally derived cap, gown and hood worn by graduates on degree day, the only conspicuous consequence of three years or more of poverty, boredom or frivolity, or a combination of two or more of these, but not altogether guaranteeing lack of capacity or achievement

academic freedom: *n.*   (i) principle of university governance by which the more senior mislead, exploit and persecute the more junior without external hindrance: marginally preferable to the same privilege bestowed on Government
(ii) freedom

academic politics: *n.*   the most potent spur to activity in universities and colleges, exhibited with precision in 'Microcosmographia Academica' by F. M. Cornford, Bowes and Bowes, 1908, than which nothing more need, or indeed can, be said

academician: *n.*   one who is recognized by others in a learned institution to be one of themselves

access: *n.*   right, privilege, leave or means of entry or approach to an institution or situation: demagogues may feign and fan indignation at restricted access somewhere so as to justify their accruing further powers and to conceal their inability or refusal to do what they alone can do to improve matters, which is to make further and better provision elsewhere

accidie: *n.*   the sin of spiritual and intellectual sloth, manifested in apathy and a sense of pointlessness: when faced by official initiatives, accidie can be resisted only with great strength of character

accountability: *n.*   doing what you are told and showing that you have done it: the only ability in teachers recognized by the Secretary of State

achievement: *n.*   something that someone has been able to do: unless this is something he has been told to do by a person in authority, the formal education system cannot recognize or accommodate it

acoustics: *n.*   the science of sound, aptly applied to speeches, lectures and the like when other qualities are present in traces too small for study

acronym: *n.*   a word made up of the initial letters of a group of words usually forming a title, often hit upon before the title itself: the author of the present lexicon once thought that the ideal acronym for a pressure group would be NAG'M, from which it was but a step to the foundation of the National Association of Governors and Managers

action research: *n.*   originally a means of tackling educational problems, now any inquiry conducted in a school or classroom, in which the research involves and implies no action, and any action is innocent of research

activism: *n.*   engagement of teachers and academics in educational politics, to be distinguished from activity, in that it consists mostly of talking, and from action, which in this context implies violence

actor: *n.*   politician professing an interest in education

actuary: *n.*   one who calculates the precise point at which a teacher's need for insurance becomes such that no company will supply it

addition: *n.*   taking one thing with another, mystified into the first process of arithmetic

administration: *n.*   the whole duty of schools since 1988

administrator: *n.*   one who can keep busy without doing anything

admissions number: *n.*   the means by which popular schools reject unattractive children

adolescence: *n.*   condition of the human young as a cure for which secondary education was designed by the Hadow Committee in 1926: an example of the truth that educational problems are rarely solved, merely superseded

advantage: *n.*   a better position, a boon: those who have gained it have usually taken it

advertising jingle: *n.*   literature on a par with any poem, or even all of the poems, by John Donne, according to postmodernist academics

adviser: *n.*   once an official appointed by a local education authority to help teachers, now an official appointed by a local education authority to pass on to schools the oppressions visited on it by the Government

aegis: *n.*   sponsorship or protection, originally the shield of Zeus, in the form of a goatskin, which may be allegorical

aegrotat: *n.*   degree awarded in exchange for a doctor's certificate

aesthetics: *n.*   the philosophy of beauty and taste in art: since art has now so far progressed as no longer to require either beauty or taste, the subject is purely historical

affection: *n.*   a protean quality in the absense of which education is impossible

affirmative action: *n.*   policy for equalizing qualification without equalizing achievement

age: *n.*   (i) the time since a person was born, identifiable with precision and useless for educational purposes
   (ii) the first of the three legal criteria for the suitability of a child's education (see ability and aptitude) and the only one that can be identified; but see (i) above

ageism: *n.*   a fundamental principle in the organization of education, leading to discrimination against the young, the mature, the middle-aged and the old, depending on the circumstances

agency: *n.*   administrative body invented by civil servants to do what they want while shielding Ministers from blame and themselves from the inconvenience that this would otherwise occasion

agenda: *n.*   (i) 'fit, meet and requiring to be done' (Kennedy), used of a list of items to be considered at a meeting of staff or governors of a school: an item may be important or time-consuming but not both
   (ii) self interest or strong concern, something pursued by people one disapproves of, often in a sly and secret way

aggression: *n.*   culpable and punishable behaviour in the weak: in the strong it is called power and is revered

agree: *v.*   be of the same opinion, concur: teachers, like others working collaboratively, think that agreement depends upon avoiding misunderstanding; on the contrary, misunderstanding is essential, since if people really understood one another they would never agree

aim: *n.*   action of pointing or directing at something, distinguishable from objective, the thing pointed or directed at: hopelessly muddled in the phrase 'aims and objectives' where the former is a synonym for the latter, inviting a futile dispute as to which is the more comprehensive

aims and objectives: *n.pl.*   popular method of planning based on the assumption that if you say where you want to go you can plan your route without knowing where you are starting from

algebra: *n.*   arithmetic with unknown numbers

algorithm: *n.*   problem solving without judgement, ideal for computers (cf. heuristics)

alienation: *n.*   feeling that one is a thing, not a person, without place or power in a society or organization, the consequence of excessive political, bureaucratic or industrial control, of which English education has been unaccountably deprived until recently

allegory: *n.*   literally, otherwise; an extended parable, designed to delight as well as enlighten, located by Mrs Malaprop on the banks of the Nile (R. Sheridan)

allergy: *n.* exaggerated reaction to an external stimulus: militancy is a kind of hay fever

alma mater: *n.* embarrassing term (literally 'bountiful mother') for school, college or university, used by those whose maturation the institution has arrested

altitude sickness: *n.* affliction of one occupying the high moral ground

ambition: *n.* (i) hunger for a higher place, sharpened by a suspicion that one is inadequate in the place one has
(ii) in a career an effective substitute for talent
(iii) that which persuades people that since they want to climb they must be prepared to creep

analogy: *n.* similarity: argument by analogy can be suggestive but is dangerous when used by dolts, since one element of similarity can not imply others; for example, to treat schools as businesses, because they are both organisations using money to mismanage schools

analysis: *n.* examining in discrete detail, valued in old-fashioned English education, requiring precision, clarity and criticality, respect for evidence, awareness of exceptions or counter-evidence and suspension of judgement, having the effect of inhibiting its beneficiaries from saying or doing anything at all

ancillary: *n.* non-teaching assistant in primary school, from the Latin ancilla, a little female servant

anthropology: *n.* study of peoples, societies and cultures wrongly thought by its practitioners to be odder than their own

anthropomorphism: *n.*   attributing human intelligence, consciousness, feelings and purposes to Governments, bureaucracies and corporations

anti-intellectual: *adj.*   of a prevalent attitude in progressive education expressed in child-centredness and in traditional education expressed in memorizing and repetition

antonym: *n.*   a word of contrary meaning to another, not to be confused with its opposite: the antonym of nonsense is sense, its opposite is likely to be another nonsense

anxiety: *n.*   uncertainty, agitation and dread, induced by inadequates in charge as a means of control

apostrophe: *n.*   (i) sign of omission or possession, usually omitted when required and inserted when not
   (ii) interruption in a discourse to address a particular person, a digression that is the better part of valour

appeal: *n.*   (i) futile example of bureaucratic overkill, offering endless second-guessing of routine judgements and decisions: apt for questions of life and death but not for the mere pursuit of happiness, about which there can be no agreement
   (ii) attempt to secure justice for individuals when this can be done only at the cost of injustice to others, as in admissions to or exclusion from schools

apperception: *n.*   theory of learning that describes it as the accumulation of new ideas or mental states to a store of old ones, presumably until the student's mind gloriously overflows

application: *n.*   use, relevance, request, bid, diligence or salve: the application of an application, if submitted with application, is an application for wounded feelings

appointment: *n.*   (i) mistake made by an appointing committee

(ii) in universities, the result of a committee's recognition of congenial prejudices in an applicant and accepting the judgement of others, like book publishers and journal editors, on the quality of his/her research, never considering whether he/she might have something worthwhile to say to students or might contribute to the intellectual coherence of their courses

appraisal: *n.*   a means of matching a rating of the performance of individual teachers against that of some ideal teacher, with a view to discovering that no teacher is ideal, so allowing all teachers to be hectored, bullied and vilified: one of the many management fads imposed upon education after being given up elsewhere as time-wasting, demoralizing and futile, the damage it does is concentrated in its first year, after which it becomes routine and inconsequential

apprentice: *n.*   one who is expected to learn by watching and imitating, showing what he has learned by making or doing something (cf. student)

apprenticeship: *n.*   lying metaphor, used in universities to excuse the exploitation of ill-rewarded graduate students in teaching and research

aptitude: *n.*   the third criterion for the suitability of a child's education (see age and ability): since it is not identifiable, the chief purpose of educational policy is to see that it does not arise

aptitude test: *n.*   a test designed to test whether the person tested can do what the test tests

arithmetic: *n.*   the manipulation of numbers: the third of the 'basics' (q.v.) or what used to be known as the three Rs (q.v. and see reading and writing), essential to children in primary schools and of little use thereafter (but see mental arithmetic)

art: *n.*   (i) the creation of beautiful, wonderful or significant things
   (ii) daubs by primary school children or chimpanzees, much revered but no better than those of many modern artists

art history: *n.*   numbing by painters (M. Burgess)

art school: *n.*   institution for the deskilling of those with a talent for painting or sculpture

artificial intelligence: *n.*   parody of human intelligence in computer programs, earnestly sought by the artificially intelligent

arts: *n.pl.*   non-scientific branches of knowledge, sometimes involving imagination and creativity, except when studied academically

AS level: *n.*   an attempt to remedy the futility of examinations for those aged 16 and 18 by having one at 17 as well

assembly: *n.*   meeting of a whole school at the beginning of the day, providing an inadequate substitute for the statutory act of worship in that it normally lacks the sin, shame and sentimentality that a truly Christian event requires

assessment: *n.*   (i) an activity which is said to reveal what a person knows or can do but which in practice records what part of an assigned task the person assessed cannot perform: no method of assessment has been devised which accommodates what people actually know, and since all assessments grossly underestimate the knowledge, understanding and capability of those assessed they are of little use for educational purposes

(ii) the aparatus for comparing, grading and tabulating pupils and students in a formal education system, in which a perverted notion of fairness requires that they all attempt the same performance: the idea of specifying what qualities and capacities the performance is meant to reveal and asking the students to display these in their own idiosyncratic ways is too much for educators, so assessment invariably stultifies the majority

assiduity: *n.*   useful characteristic which can either enhance talent or, more often, substitute for it

assignment: *n.*   task: an example of the educational habit of never using one syllable where three will do

asterisk: *n.*   a small stellar character, a short row of which primly amounts to a euphemism

attainment: *n.*   the point someone has reached on a scale of marks awarded for performance at a predetermined task: no attainment is satisfactory because there is always an actual or potential attainment that is better

attendance: *n.*   that relationship of children with school that parents think it their whole legal duty to secure: if they were to perform their real duty, which is to see that their children are suitably educated, either at school or otherwise, formal education could scarcely survive

attention: *n.* that which pupils are required to pay, a kind of tax on school attendance

attention span: *n.* measure of ability to concentrate, said by journalists to be shrinking in the populace to excuse its virtual disappearance in themselves

audiovisual aids: *n.pl.* devices appealing to two senses rather than to the mind

autarchy: *n.* a treacherous word meaning both self-rule and dictatorship: education is meant to encourage the former and inhibit the latter, and it is funny how often it seems to do the opposite

authority: *n.* (i) accepted ability to act, command, control or judge, distinguishable from power and force, now so tenuous as to leave the latter as the only and ineffective means of social cohesion: in schools the authority of teachers has been diminished not only as part of the social trend but also by deliberate acts of Government and the caperings of unionized fatheads; and as other sanctions have been ruled out by legislation and litigation the purposeful order of most schools can come only from miraculous professionalism

(ii) once a guarantee of the certainty of knowledge: the authority might be of a person (the Pope), an institution (the Church) or books (the Bible, the early Fathers or the Classics), but none of these could convince once people started thinking for themselves

autobiography: *n.* a book comprising the fantasies of its author and malicious gossip about others

autodidact: *n.* a deplorable person who gains knowledge or capability without benefit of teaching by another: his chief failing, that of believing that what he happens to know is more significant than what he does not know, is one that he shares with the scholar

average: *n.* a number obtained by dividing the sum of a number of numbers by the total number of numbers: for an average to exist at all, some numbers must be larger than average and some smaller, except in educational policy which requires all numbers to be above average (the authorities are thinking of legs: since a small number of people have only one leg or fewer, the average number of legs per person is slightly less than two, so almost everyone has more than the average number of legs)

baby: *n.* (i) what new parents think they have: what they actually have is a teenager, and the teenage starts at the age of eight and ends at the age of 28; if you are lucky

(ii) item to be retained when disposing of bathwater, a principle unknown to reformers

baccalaureate: *n.* qualification which, because foreign, must be better than anything English

backache: *n.* the one undeniable consequence of English secondary education, having lifelong effects; brought about by long sedentary hours interspersed with movement burdened by bags containing half their owner's body weight in books and equipment

background: *n.* part of a scene furthest from the viewer, or in a picture that which seems so; used for a person's social class, education, training or experience, or for the circumstances, social, historical or technical, that explain or lead to something, by people who are too lazy or confused to say what they mean

backlog: *n.* large log which, being at the back of a fireplace, does not easily burn away: since wood fires have gone out of fashion, people think backlog means arrears of work

bar chart: *n.* patronizing attempt to make statistics palatable by packaging them like chocolate

basics: *n.pl.* what everybody not at school thinks those at school ought to 'concentrate' on, consisting of the three Rs of reading, writing and arithmetic (q.v.), in the hope that there can be no possible pleasure involved (cf. frills): 'success' in the basics is demanded particularly of infants in England even though countries where children do rather better at them regard starting so young as an ignorant barbarism

beacon school: *n.* one that offers signal encouragement to conflagrations elsewhere

beatitudes: *n.pl.* blessings uttered by a leader, as in Matthew 5.3–11: those of a Secretary of State to teachers might be as follows

Blessed are the poor in spirit for I made them so

Blessed are they that mourn for they shall have plenty to mourn about

Blessed are the meek for they shall be ordered about

Blessed are they who hunger and thirst after righteousness, for they shall never be fed

Blessed are the merciful for they shall let me get away with it

Blessed are the pure in heart for they shall never suspect me

Blessed are the peacemakers for they shall mitigate the strife I cause

Blessed are they who are persecuted for I intend to go on persecuting

bedlam: *n.* normal consequence of the belief that the interests of individual pupils should always come before those of pupils generally

behaviour: *n.* the way a child conducts himself, inevitably unsatisfactory and requiring management, modification and therapy

behaviour management: *n.* application of the stick, the carrot or both

behaviour modification: *n.* inadequate substitute for thrashing, based on the same assumptions but having a different end in view

behaviour therapy: *n.* treating people's fears by repeated frights and their vices by punishment

behavioural science: *n.* study of the inducements needed for animals to press buttons or levers, make noises or run through doors or mazes

behaviourism: *n.* theory that human beings can be understood without the notion of a mind

bell: *n.* chief governing principle of secondary education

bell-shaped curve: *n.*   graphic representation of the evident truth that in respect of any characteristic most people are much like each other, with a few having notably more or less of it than the rest: picturing the bell-shaped curve reminds us of the fatuity of grades and other classifications

best practice: *n.*   (i) teaching method which officials wish to make compulsory
(ii) what successful teachers do: requiring others, who are different, to do the same is usually futile and, if imposed, damaging

bibliography: *n.*   (i) study of every aspect of books except their content
(ii) list of books by or about a person or relating to a subject appended to a thesis to imply that its vacuity is scholarly

bibliophile: *n.*   one who likes, buys and collects books without necessarily wanting to read them

biddable: *adj.*   condition in which formal education is designed to leave all students

bien-pensant: *adj.*   right-thinking or orthodox, that is more likely to be wrong-thinking

binary digit: *n.*   a bit longer

binary policy: *n.*   vain attempt by a politician, A. Crosland, and a civil servant, T. Weaver, to get people in higher education to think what they were doing as a basis for rational organization, mindlessly abandoned in 1992

binary scale: *n.* counting in the base two, instead of the more usual ten, inflicted on infants some years ago as part of the 'new maths', amusing for a moment but pointless otherwise: computers work with a binary scale, but they know no better

biology: *n.* the study of living organisms, usually conducted on dead ones and through books: the only branch of interest to adolescents is that concerning themselves, and this is so successfully eschewed in schools as to leave them for the rest of their lives at the mercy of their doctors

bit: *n.* single digit of binary notation, 0 or 1; the smallest unit of information: the point of a needle on which dance the angels of calculation and communication

black: *adj.* having no hue, dark: misapplied as a description of skin colour, where it is no more accurate than white: the distinction between the two is of no importance and when insisted upon causes nothing but trouble

blackboard: *n.* hard, dark, vertical surface to be covered by teachers with chalked words, diagrams or figures for copying by students: now largely replaced by whiteboards and markers, projectors and acetates or flipcharts that contain the same old stuff and have the same purpose

blame: *v.* (i) attribute failure, neglect and error to somebody else, hugely popular among those paid to carry responsibility

(ii) censure someone else for not preventing the evil conequences of one's own actions, as when

Governments insist that school pitches be sold off and then complain of the neglect of sport

blue book: *n.*   report by a Royal Commission or Departmental Committee, arrived at after two or three years' public discussion, setting out the changes now generally acceptable, a basis for stable reform now largely discarded

bluestocking: *n.*   disparaging term for a woman with intellectual interests, now obsolete since both men and women have come to see that such women are common enough to be borne without sneering

board school: *n.*   institution established by a school board, not to be confused with bored school which is a tautology

boarder: *n.*   pupil who lives at school, taking his chance on physical as well as intellectual nourishment

boarding school: *n.*   (i) secure training centre for the hitherto uncriminal children of the rich, on no account to be confused with board school
   (ii) institution invented by novelists writing for children

body language: *n.*   posture and gestures conveying meaning, emotion, disposition or purpose, when conscious better known as acting, when unconscious unreliable

bog-standard: *adj.*   of the quality of a mercenary in the Prime Minister's office

book: *n.*   the most advanced technology available for learning, all vaunted substitutes having been found less efficient

bookish: *adj.*   fond of reading, a term of opprobrium applied to the young as soon as they begin to enjoy doing what the Secretary of State and all right-thinking persons say is the most important thing for children to do

booklearning: *n.*   knowledge gained from reading, an inadequate substitute for learning, which involves thinking and experience, but all that is required by examinations

booklist: *n.*   recommended books listed for students at the beginning of a course: students despair unnecessarily at the length of such lists, not realizing that in education books are not to be read but used, plundered for information and ideas and above all put on other lists, this time of references

boredom: *n.*   (i) society ruled by a bore (as in kingdom, officialdom)
    (ii) signal that it is time to neglect what is being offered in favour of something else in the hope of learning something: unhappily not all the substitues are benign, nor is all the subsequent learning beneficial

box: *n.*   a little printed square for putting a tick in, the peak of intellectual effort demanded of inspectors and appraisers

boy: *n.*   male child, a creature for and with whom little can be done, baffling even the great Dr T. Arnold who said, as he took on Rugby School, 'My object will be, if possible, to form Christian men, for Christian boys I can scarcely hope to make'

Boyle's law: *n.*   the principle that the pressure of a gas varies inversely with its volume at constant temperature, refuted by Blunkett's principle according to which when things hot up politically the speeches of a Secretary of State are both longer and more oppressive

brains: *n.pl.*   effective substitute for schooling: 'I did not have much education, so I had to use my brains' (B. Shankley)

brainstorm: *n.*   mental aberration, but see brainstorming

brainstorming: *ger.*   gathering of people in a group to multiply mental aberrations, in the hope of hitting on usable ideas, rational solutions and sensible proposals

brainwave: *n.*   (i) sudden bright idea: in most people this is the beginning of a thoughtful and productive process, in Government it is taken to render such a process otiose
   (ii) mental activity detectable by an electro-encephalogram

bribe: *n.*   inducement, usually monetary, to do or accept something against one's better judgement, widely employed by modern governments, characterized by the lack of any other benefit to the person bribed (see performance-related pay)

bright: *adj.*   animated, quick to respond; not to be confused with clever and especially not with intelligent

broad and balanced: *adj.*   the legal requirement for a school curriculum: since the National Curriculum, which schools are bound to follow, is narrow, partial and ephemeral, the requirement can be met by schools only in the time they can free from it

broke: *adj.*   condition of something not necessary before some reformer proposes to fix it

broken home: *n.*   unhappy family which one member has left in order to minimize misery, said to make its children unteachable

bullying: *ger.*   intimidating or persecuting a weaker person, reprehensible in children but normal in politicians, officials and other very righteous people: children have been perfecting their technique in it by a close study of inspections

bureaubabble: *n.*   the language of organizations, officialese: its chief characteristics are circumlocution and the use of words that are so general as to be empty of meaning, its object to by-pass reality, defy understanding and thus inhibit objection

bureaucracy: *n.*   (i) government by those who are simultaneously sedentary and pedestrian
  (ii) suppression secured by sheer weight of paper

buzz word: *n.*   cant term of vague but favourable import, used to preempt objection, argument or intelligent discussion, like standards, inclusion

byte: *n.*   eight bits (q.v.), enough to make a character on a computer: these days what counts as news is that 'bytes dog man' (M. Burgess)

caffeine: *n.*   soft drug the harmful over-indulgence in which by the young is the next object of the world capitalist conspiracy

calculator: *n.*   (i) device for relieving the chore of arithmetic, which may thereby either destroy or enhance the understanding of number, but nobody knows which
(ii) electronic device which does not calculate, since only human beings do that, any more than a clock tells the time: an abacus, a slide-rule or a logarithmic table is clearly a thing with which one calculates, not a thing which calculates itself, and the same is true of a calculator, except to those who believe in magic

calculus: *n.*   mathematical technique for investigating the effects on a system of small controlled changes on a single relevant variable, highly desirable but unknown in educational policy

Cambridge: *pr.n.*   '... the best preparatory school for Oxford...' (O. Wilde)

campus: *n.*   originally a games park or drill area and hence the grounds of a university

candidate: *n.*   applicant for a post, from the Latin for 'white', a colour nobody looks his best in

capability: *n.*   that which enables one to act successfully in circumstances where one lacks competence

career: *n.*   concept fatal in schools, in which there are no careers, since one is either a teacher or a headteacher, and the institution is collegial or nothing: a 'career' structure in teaching, involving intermediate and artificial posts, is a device for paying most teachers too little by offering some a little more; otherwise a career in education requires the desertion of schools and children for administering, advising, inspecting or going into Parliament

caring community: *n.*   school in perpetual disorder

carrot and stick: *n.*   principle of management favoured by those who can cope with no organization more complex than a donkey cart: interestingly, everything described as a carrot, like performance-related pay, turns out to be a stick

catachresis: *n.*   misuse of words, as in saying disinterested for uninterested: in the parable of the man fallen among thieves, the Samaritan was disinterested, the priest and the Levite uninterested (Luke 10. 30–37)

catastrophism: *n.*   theory of creation by sudden and logically unrelated acts, no longer believed about the earth but still apt for the education system

catechism: *n.*   traditional model of formal instruction, where the student memorizes and repeats standard answers to predetermined questions, usually without interest in the questions or understanding of the answers

cause: *n.*   (i) that which produces an effect
   (ii) position adopted or advanced, whatever the effect produced, if any

censor: *n.*   heroic person who seeks out anything that may deprave or corrupt himself, in order to suppress it for the protection of others

censorship: *n.*   vain attempt to stop people thinking anything that might astonish, bewilder or upset a policeman

centralization: *n.*   administrative principle according to which the Secretary of State does everything, and nothing can be done unless done or ordered by him: it has brought empires to ruin and will do the same for English education should teachers and parents come to accept that it exists

certainty: *n.*   a thing which people earnestly desire and cannot attain, hence the existence of manufactured substitutes like religion, traditional science and common sense

certificate: *n.*   official form showing that one is born, married, dead or academically approved of

chair: *n.*   (i) chief support of a university professor, not to be confused with a seat of learning: many people have pointed out that however prestigious the chair, the holder is always sitting on his own bottom

(ii) an academic or administrative distinction held, rather than sat in, except as in the following American obituary: 'He occupied the chair of applied electricity at one of our most notable institutions and died in harness'

chalk: *n.*   white soft earthy limestone once thought uniquely efficacious in intruding facts into the minds of children, sometimes in conjunction with talk, though how this occurred was never explained or understood

change: *n.*   political substitute for improvement

charisma: *n.*   personal or *ex officio* attractiveness that enables one without further qualities to influence others, usually for evil, and even when for general good to the others' particular harm

chattering classes: *n.pl.* people who often talk about politics, art or ideas, as contrasted with non-chatterers who talk about popstars and football

chautauqua: *n.* a summer school, named after the place in the United States where the first one was said to have taken place: in England it had better be called a dartington

chauvinism: *n.* the response of weak minds to lessons in loyalty, manliness and other secondary virtues

chemistry: *n.* school subject largely devoted to cooking

child: *n.* human being before puberty, thought to be specially malleable and thus vulnerable to determined manipulation by Secretaries of State and other bigots, who cannot see that the genes win in the long run

child-centred: *adj.* characterized by worship of the child instead of the Secretary of State and by weak-minded reverence for what the child says, does or produces

children's interests: *n.pl.* the basis of child-centred education: many children lead such intellectually impoverished lives that they have few interests worth the name, and a few have interests that are malign, so such things as personal experiences and activities and such values as spontaneity may be useful servants of learning but bad masters

chimera: *n.*   a monster and a myth, like a plan for increased spending on education announced by a Chancellor of the Exchequer

choice: *n.*   properly a preference, but the word is used by politicians when introducing arrangements whereby some, usually most, people are denied something previously taken for granted and thus made worse off than before

Christianity: *n.*   the state religion of England, according to education law, which requires its worship and teaching in schools, by which children learn that a developed faith may be at odds with the precepts and practices of its nominal founder

church school: *n.*   school which adheres to some view of Christianity and which admits either the children of those who say that they share that view or other children whom it expects to proselytize: both kinds have a desired air of social and academic respectability, and the chance that thay might encourage real bigotry is probably small

circular: *n.*   boring and outmoded means by which the DfES used to explain legislation or policy, recently superseded: DfES communications now come in five 'functional categories', viz 'Information: "Here's what we have in mind", Consultation: "Here's how we plan to go about it. What do you think?", Guidance: "Here's what you have to do to make it work", Practice: "Here are the tools to do it", Data collection: "Questions we want you to answer",' all of which places the DfES securely beyond the reach of parody

citizenship: *n.*   school subject derived from a well-meaning attempt to interest pupils in personal responsibility and democratic values, hopeless since school denies them experience of these things and has of late denied this to their teachers as well

class: *n.*   (i) group to which things are taught collectively which cannot be learnt except individually

(ii) fatuous division of those graduating: in the nature of the case there must be more difference in achievement between those within a class than between those on either side of the border between one class and another

(iii) social division invented by snobs, straight and inverted, and refined with great labour by the Government statistical service

classics: *n.pl.*   (i) great works of thought or feeling, either ancient or more recent, but never contemporary; once the whole basis and content of education but now apparently dispensable

(ii) Latin and ancient Greek language and literature, once widely blamed for education's failure to prepare children for usefulness in and enjoyment of adult life: Latin and Greek have since been abandoned but the children remain ill-prepared

(iii) a discipline in which every word was meant to be scrupulously weighed and savoured, the decay of which has rendered academic writing uncouth and political rhetoric crass

classroom: *n.*   bleak chamber in which some thirty people sooner or later accept that one of them is in charge

clever: *adj.*   adroit, skillful, ingenious, a characteristic useful at school but fatal to a career thereafter

cliché: *n.*   from the French for stereotype, a phrase ready-made or off-the-peg; useful for speechmakers who can make their minds blank and let the clichés flood through, determining their thoughts and concealing their meaning from their hearers and themselves: 'This is no time for clichés; the hand of history is on our shoulder' (T. Blair)

cluster group: *n.*   a number of primary schools associated with a secondary school, on the false assumptions that the latter has something to offer the former and that the only function of each stage of education is to serve the next

coaching: *ger.*   preparing someone for a performance or contest: in schools, seeking to secure by repeated practice better results in tests which are said to be proof against this

code of practice: *n.*   new means of bureaucratic control, filling the gap between endless legislation and limitless guidance, not itself having the force of law but from which deviation might be held by Secretaries of State to be unreasonable, thus enabling them to direct compliance

coeducation: *n.*   accommodating boys and girls in the same school, normal outside England and in English schools for the working and lower middle classes but suspect among the old-fashioned rich and those who have noticed that girls and boys develop at different rates

coffee: *n.*   beverage the quality of which is an indicator of staffroom morale

cognitive psychology: *n.* theories of learning relying on an analogy between minds and computers, often suggestive but of limited relevance in education, since minds are active and computers only metaphorically so

college: *n.* once a self-governing community of scholars, now an agency of the DfES

college of education: *n.* training college (q.v.) with aspirations to educate teachers of all kinds of children (obs.)

College of Teachers: *n.* the only extant hope of a professional institution and learned society for teachers, which teachers might just be persuaded not to neglect into oblivion

colligative properties: *n.pl.* in physics, those properties which are so linked that if one of them is known the others are predictable: in education the syndrome appears, for example, in the views of the politically correct (D. Mendel)

colloquium: *n.* originally an informal gathering for chat, now an elaborately organized academic conference on a specialist subject, valued only for the opportunity it gives for informal chat

commitment: *n.* quality demanded of others by those in charge, always rationally withheld: 'Think of an English breakfast of eggs and bacon: the hen was involved, the pig was committed' (I. Campbell)

committee: *n.* a body established by the Secretary of State to produce wisdom: since only individuals are capable of judgement, committees have to use substitutes, so those representing interest groups use horsetrading, those of experts use backscratching, political ones find the lowest common denominator, and so on; and because a committee can have no conscience, there is nothing that it cannot be persuaded to do

common room: *n.*   sitting room in an institution where staff or students (rarely both together) relax, chat and thus educate each other (cf. staff room)

communication: *n.*   originally a mutual enterprise, from Latin *communicare*, to share, but now a mere imparting and transmitting: communicators care only that their message has 'got across', that it has been passively received, and the more complex the means of communication, the less communication in the old sense takes place

community: *n.*   empty abstraction with a hint of spurious comfort, as in care in the community, also used in a similar sense in school, academic or minority community

competence: *n.*   (i) enough to live on: a modest ambition in teachers, sometimes realized
(ii) originally general ability, now debased to mean a tested performance in a particular and limited task, preferably one taken from a list drawn up by a bore

competences: *n.pl.*   concept behind a management fad from the last century, now seen to be inapt for business and bureaucracy and always so when applied to children and their teachers, hence much favoured by officials

competition: *n.*   (i) the meat of avarice and the poison of altruism

(ii) in education a principle that favours those who are good at tests and examinations, if nothing else

(iii) in a newspaper a spurious obstacle to entry into a worthless lottery

(iv) any scramble for scarce places in schools or universities, which theory insists brings general benefits and experience reveals to be deeply debilitating

compliance: *n.*   the chief requirement from those in charge which, when granted, happily hastens their downfall

comprehension: *n.*   (i) mental grasp, act of or capacity for understanding

(ii) test to determine whether a student's interpretation of a piece of writing is as crass as the examiner's

(iii) that beyond which educational policy is often found to be

comprehensive school: *n.*   in England a secondary school which admits the children of its neighbourhood without tests or conditions: in other countries a comprehensive school is called a school

compromise: *n.*   stalling between two fools (S. Fry)

computer: *n.*   electronic device which does not compute (and see calculator) but is rather an elaborate machine which has been so programmed as to enable people to handle and store data, from all over the world if required: a serviceable drudge but a destructive master

concentration: *n.*   mental application or complete attention, a prerequisite of learning, impossible to those in most systems of formal education

concept: *n.*   abstract idea, once much worried over in the philosophy of education to little productive effect: a group of psychologists once debated all day whether to throw a Christmas party for a mothers' and toddlers' club which they ran and decided against it on the ground that the toddlers would not have the concept of a party

conditioning: *ger.*   (i) tricking a person or animal into responding to something, say a bell, hitherto accompanying something else, like food, but now on its own: the relation of this to education was always tenuous, and since the effect quickly wears off, like conditioning in hair, it is clear that conditioning, in the claimed sense of producing significant change, is a myth

(ii) theory of learning based on (i) above, offered in two forms: classical conditioning claims to secure desired responses to particular stimuli, and operant conditioning reinforces the desired responses by subsequent reward, even to the point of controlling a whole learning environment to make the desired responses more likely, a theory to which many teachers cling whether it works or not

conference: *n.*   formal meeting, sometimes lasting several days, so organized as to give participants the opportunity to speak without the obligation to listen

confidence: *n.*   one of the most necessary qualities in a student, which teachers maintain in the teeth of the formal system: not to be confused with arrogance, which is its antonym

conjugation: *n.*   what happens to a verb when its form changes to indicate its person, number, tense, voice and mood, as in swim, swam, swum or am, are, is: it survives in English but in an etiolated form, so that foreign languages, as presently taught, remain beyond the grasp of English children

consciousness: *n.*   a condition which, according to the current state of physical, neurological and medical science, cannot be explained so must needs be explained away

consensus: *n.*   general agreement, the search for which ensures that a desirable thing can be done only when it would now be better to do something else

conservative: *n.*   (i) one who believes that existing evils should be revered, as distinct from a reformer, who wishes to invent new ones, and a radical, who prefers those abolished in 1970
    (ii) one with a well-developed tolerance for the misery of others (C. Heilbrun)

consistency: *n.*   quality of the circumstances in which, however seemingly unpromising, children tend to thrive: today's children find themselves dealing with parents, peers, schools, the mass media and much else, most of which are at odds with each other

conspiracy: *n.*   typical mode of organization of a profession in its relation to the public: teachers, having become a profession only recently, are as yet unskilled in its mysteries

consult: *v.*   to seek approval for a course of action already decided upon so as to reassure the perpetrator that he can proceed with impunity

consultation: *n.*   activity undertaken for the benefit of those consulting, not those consulted, specifically a communication from the DfES containing a questionnaire designed to elicit support for what it has decided to do (see circular)

consumer: *n.*   person viewed as a locust or gannet, an inapt and demeaning metaphor in education

continuous assessment: *n.*   periodic assessment: the practice requires the presentation of material in trivializing bits and is destructive of understanding

converted, the: *n.pl.*   the only people worth preaching to

copy: *v.*   reproduce the work of another, reprehensible when the work copied is that of another student, praiseworthy when it is that of a teacher: producing faithful copies is the chief purpose of instruction

copybook: *n.*   (obs.) book of examples of penmanship for imitation and blots

core subject: *n.*   science, maths or English in primary schools, mostly thrown away later like the core of an apple

corporal punishment: *n.*   wizened euphemism for flogging

corporate language: *n.*   words employed by modern tyrants in place of a worked-out theory of tyranny, as in casualize, downsize, outsource, reengineer, reposition, restructure, segment, streamline: their use is the harbinger of a new oppression

correlation: *n.*   statistical coincidence

cosmetic: *adj.*   the necessary attribute and prime purpose of Government policy

cost-benefit analysis: *n.* an assessment of the gains and losses to society of a scheme as well as the costs and revenues it might generate, never applied to education, lest it should appear that extra spending there would in social terms be cheap at the price

cost-effective: *adj.* offering a good return on outlay, valid and measurable when both are financial, vacuous and mischievous otherwise

counselling: *n.* psychotherapy for the sane: it used to be called guidance and counselling, but counsellors have sensibly given up guidance

course: *n.* (i) a hunt by hounds relying on sight rather than smell
(ii) prescribed number of lessons or lectures, or the content thereof, through which children or others are pursued within sight of a teacher
(iii) package tour, with guide, of an area more enticing in the brochure than in reality

coursework: *n.* piece of writing or artifact produced for assessment and for little other purpose within the timed part of a course

crackdown: *n.* politician's answer to a sense of public indignation at something he cannot alter

cram: *v.* prepare for an examination by hasty memorizing, the most efficient way of gaining a pass which is all that matters

crash: *n.* collapse, collision or loud noise: when used as an adjective in crash course it implies an attempted short cut to learning, involving much of the original definition

creativity: *n.*   power to create, originality of thought, inventiveness, imagination: a rare and precious gift, vulgarized and discredited by its attribution to any activity, however banal, wearisome or unprofitable, of a worshipped child

crèche: *n.*   day nursery where academic parents leave their young children in order to turn their own nurturing instincts and abilities on their students, except in the case of those without such abilities

credit: *n.*   (i) a pass in part of a course, when used as currency to gain exemption from part of another course, thus rendering both courses incoherent
    (ii) a pass with nobs on

credit accumulation: *n.*   academic avarice

credit transfer: *n.*   being excused part of one course because one has completed part of another

criterion: *n.*   substitute for judgement: the plural is criteria, but television presenters make their contribution to illiteracy by using this as if it were the singular, as they do with bacteria, data, media and phenomena and would do with any other Greek or Latin words if they knew them

critic: *n.*   one who serves the public good by doing individuals harm

criticism: *n.*   the duty of a teacher toward any offering from a pupil or student: not to be confused with making an assessment, but involving appreciation of what was done, decision as to whether it was worth doing and generous judgement on whether it was done well, designed to raise achievement rather than to impose standards

crucifixion: *n.* cheering ornament in Catholic schools

culture: *n.* (i) that which makes possible the social, political and economic arrangements in a population, the only thing that one can reach for when people turn to guns

(ii) that which makes life worth living for individuals: in neither this nor the preceding sense is it much accommodated in the school curriculum

(iii) a term that, when qualified by another, implies the opposite of the meanings above, as in youth culture, yob culture, pop culture, blame culture, canteen culture, culture of violence, culture of racism, all of which have the character of fashion accessories

culture-free: *adj.* oddly desirable quality of some tests, ensuring that they cannot register any particular achievement or capability

cultured: *adj.* artificially grown

curiosity: *n.* quality in children which it is important to crush lest it kill a cat

current affairs: *n.pl.* adultery in politics, films, pop music or sport, the preferred content of newspapers

curriculum: *n.* the systematic provision of unwanted answers to unasked questions (K. Popper)

curve: *n.* (i) graphical representation of a mathematical function, even when it is a straight line

(ii) a straight line from a politician, produced as in cricket by spin

custom: *n.*   community-based error

cybernetics: *n.*   the science of control systems, unknown in politics and public administration, where control systems are unscientific, not to say crude, maladroit and destructive

cynicism: *n.*   the faith of the faithless: it was a cynic who said that the foundation of every state was the education of its youth

dame school: *n.*   the beginning, so we are told, of English popular education, lastingly influential in that pupils still call female teachers 'Miss'

data: *n.pl.*   (i) literally, things given: a misnomer, since what we know is not given but made, as in facta (facts)
   (ii) collections of numbers never quite adding up to knowledge

data collection: *n.*   (i) mindless activity invented for the employment of sociologists
   (ii) the fifth category of communication from the DfES, requiring answers to tomfool questions which are asked only because the DfES can think of nothing for the moment in the other four categories (see circular)

database: *n.*   vast amount of information held on a computer, systematically arranged so that it can be found and manipulated immediately, seldom consulted or used and if used inconsequential

day school: *n.*   school from which regular escape is possible: homework is its revenge

de-effese: *n.*   language of the DfES, a lethal combination of bureaubabble, psychobabble, pudder, newspeak, management-speak and neo-labourisms, empty of content even when in the imperative mood

deathwish: *n.*   the urge to self-destruction which fortunately seizes governments, usually though not always before they can do too much damage; a hopeful feature of politics

debt: *n.*   the one certain consequence of a course of higher education

decadence: *n.*   decay of morality or culture, so called because it has always been taking place within the last ten years

decalogue: *n.*   ten curt exhortations together forming a code of professional conduct, called Mosaic after the inventor of the form rather than the stones on which he wrote: an example for teachers follows
1. Thou shalt have none other gods but the Secretary of State
2. Thou shalt not deal in concrete expressions but in abstractions only
3. Thou shalt not swear by, about or at the Secretary of State
4. Remember the INSET day, to keep it holy
5. Honour the Inspectorate that thy days in thy job may continue
6. Thou shalt not kill learning: the National Curriculum shall do it for thee

7. Thou shalt not commit adultery, except with sixth-formers
8. Thou shalt not steal, except in writing a postgraduate thesis
9. Thou shalt not bear false witness against a colleague, lest he tell the truth about thee
10. Thou shalt not covet repose nor recognition nor any thing that thou might reasonably expect

decency: *n.*   that which appears to be normal behaviour since indecency is less assertive and intrusive

decimals: *n.pl.*   a way of writing fractions on one rather than two lines, the numerator following a full stop or decimal point and the denominator being understood, being a power of ten: the decimal system is a triumph of simple-mindedness since it cannot accommodate useful fractions like thirds, sevenths or ninths

decimate: *v.*   reduce by one tenth: those who have never been Roman legionaries, for whom it was a random punishment, think it means to annihilate

decision: *n.*   that which decision-makers make, or more often do not make

declension: *n.*   what happens to a noun, pronoun or adjective when its form changes to indicate its case, number or gender: since it scarcely survives in English, pedagogues used to make children learn its detail in dead languages, and their ceasing to do so leaves English children baffled by the structure of any foreign language that retains it

deconstruction: *n.*   polemical academic technique that meets an argument by investigating, not its cogency, but the character of its author, identifying where the latter 'is coming from'; for example, the argument for deconstruction is flawed because its advocates are white, mainly French, middle-class males

defence mechanism: *n.*   postulated inhibitor of anxiety about one's natural urges: were such mechanisms to exist and be effective the protection of civilized life would require every second person to be a policeman

definition: *n.*   the meaning of a word or the act of attributing such meaning, in either case telling one less about the words than about the person doing the defining: if two people arguing disagree about the meaning of a word their only serviceable recourse is to use another one, since one definition leads not to clarity but only to a demand for others

democracy: *n.*   (i) form of Government, rule by the people, impossible in any organization larger than a tennis club and rare even there; in countries, it implies that the Government may be regularly changed by peaceful means, like elections, that power is checked, balanced, widely distributed and accountable, and that people may criticize and oppose what is being done to and for them: no experience of any of this is available in any formal education system

(ii) political system which peoples and individuals mistakenly believe will give them a Government they want, whereas what it can do, and this is of the essence, is to enable them to dismiss a Government that dipleases them

(iii) government by discussion, but it is only effective if you can stop people talking (C. Attlee)

democratic centralism: *n.*   the principle of organization of Soviet Communism, under which the decisions of higher bodies were absolutely binding on those below them, introduced into English education in the last quarter of the twentieth century to coincide with its final collapse in Russia

demonstrate: *v.*   (i) show, evince, explain or conjecture (ii) show, by marching or sitting down, that one does not understand politics or power: this lexicographer's mother once marched through Westminster carrying a peace-loving placard proclaiming, 'What fools we mortals be'

department: *n.*   division of a university organized to deliver instruction, normally devoid of intellectual life, partly because the academics are so specialized that they mostly communicate with people in departments elsewhere

department of education: *n.*   part of a university with the aspirations of a college of education (q.v.) now officially required to act as a training college (q.v.)

deputy head: *n.*   teacher doing the work of a headteacher when the latter is absent or present

design: *n.*   plan, as for a new or refurbished building: when used as an adjective as in design concept or design solution it indicates something dim, unworthy or meretricious

design and technology: *n.pl.*   pretentious term for the few useful accomplishments accommodated in the National Curriculum, presented so as to make proficiency in any one of them impossible: a case of terminological inflation as cookery, for example, became domestic science, then home economics and is now part of DT

desire: *n.* essential basis for learning, a fact well known to teachers but ignored in formal systems

desk: *n.* item of furniture creating the combined effects of the cage, the treadmill and the rack

despair: *n.* a giant, the owner of Doubting Castle and the husband of diffidence (after J. Bunyan), holding fully one-third of teachers in his thrall with the unstinting aid of the DfES

despond: *n.* a slough (after J. Bunyan) fed by a seepage of official material and in which teachers find themselves wallowing

detention: *n.* punishment for pupils imposing a penalty on teachers

develop: *v.* to grow, mature or otherwise improve, or to occasion improvement: much development is natural and makes possible more and different learning; some is induced, the result of learning, and teachers need to know which is which

developmental age: *n.* the stage an individual has reached in the course of maturing, which follows the same sequence in all but at different rates: critical for educational purposes and thus ignored in formal systems

deviant: *adj.* out of the ordinary, and always undesirably so

DfES: *n.* the Department for Education and Skills, a repository of ignorant power, the unaccountable often engaged in the unlawful: this is a new title for the Government department concerned with education and is as meaningful as referring to a shop for groceries and cheese (J. Pratt)

diagnostic assessment: *n.*   test

dictionary: *n.*   lexicon, but dictionary derives from mediaeval Latin, while lexicon derives from Greek, so the latter is more academic or would be if it were not one syllable shorter

didactic: *adj.*   given to excessive instruction, a deadly sin in teachers, and one officially encouraged

dilemma: *n.*   a choice betwen two equally undesirable courses, frequently found in human affairs but still giving rise to resentment in the immature

dilettante: *n.*   one who knows enough about something he likes to maximize delight, thus despised by academics and critics, though not by artists

dinner lady: *n.*   person ruining her days for a pittance so as to guarantee the social cohesion of a school and the courteous demeanour of its pupils

diploma: *n.*   piece of stiff paper more desirable than a certificate and less so than a degree, such distinctions being the essence of academic judgement

director of education: *n.*   once the person responsible for education in an area, accountable to an elected council, now an errand boy of the Secretary of State

disciple: *n.*   follower of a leader, thinker or teacher: if you wish to be thoroughly misinformed about a person's thought, ask a self-proclaimed disciple

disciplinary: *n.* of a procedure designed to ensure than any blame attaches to the person or persons lowest in the hierarchy of those responsible

discipline: *n.* (i) field of knowledge, frequently lying fallow
(ii) conditions imposed for improvement, leading sooner or later to deterioration, for example muscular growth in sportsmen goes to fat
(iii) doing what you are told, quickly
(iv) tyranny and torture

discourse: *n.* (i) the whole of reality, according to postmodernists
(ii) talk

discrimination: *n.* (i) subtle appreciation in matters of taste, or the ability to see fine distinctions
(ii) a habit of making prejudicial judgements or decisions about individuals or members of groups: deploring this gives philistines the excuse for hating (i) above

discussion: *n.* headteacher's monologue at a staff meeting

disorder: *n.* principle reason why children learn too little at school, more damaging than any particular teaching method, however batty: its causes are various, including the removal of effective sanctions against it, the destruction of respect for teachers by the Government and its agencies, the tedium of the curriculum and the faddy policy of inclusion which places teachers and pupils at the mercy of the devilish and the deranged

dissertation: *n.*   essay swollen to look like a thesis

distance learning: *n.*   the urgent and secret desire of all university administrators, offering the boon of eliminating from the campus first the students and soon thereafter the academics

diversity: *n.*   condition of being different or varied, advocated by politicians and officials when existing arrangements are consistent, satisfactory and popular, so that the circumstances of some or most people may be debased

docile: *adj.*   easy to manage, control or discipline and making no objection to being taught

doctorate: *n.*   a reward given to a postgraduate student who diligently completes some part of the work of his professor

doctrine: *n.*   principle or system of principles, less reprehensible than dogma, and inconveniently inhibiting to those in office whose urge to do something is stronger than their understanding of what they are doing

dormitory: *n.*   communal bedroom in a boarding school where the lack of privacy is vainly hoped to encourage chastity

drop-in centre: *n.*   centre for drop-outs

drop-out: *n.*   a critic of a school or college course with the courage of his convictions

drunken helot: *n.*   Spartan slave made drunk to show to the young the evils of drink, proof, if proof were needed, of the educational futility of example

dunce: *n.* one who finds it hard to learn what another insists he should by the methods the latter uses (obs., but see special needs)

duty: *n.* that which is expected of one: if the expectation has not been raised by oneself, it is a mere imposition and has no moral force

dyslexia: *n.* inability to recognize and reproduce written and printed words, not explicable by lack of application, wealth or intelligence; a condition entirely to be expected in a proportion of any population: the wonder is not that some people cannot read and write as required but that most people can

e-mail: *n.* (i) the most efficient form of delivery for junk yet devised: getting rid of this takes longer than with any other method and can incapacitate people for hours

(ii) form of communication favoured by university administrators because it precludes privacy

eclipse: *n.* occasion for mass hysteria masquerading as a thirst for knowledge

ecology: *n.* once the study of the relationship between species and their environments, now a programme for coercion of individuals in the supposed interest of the planet

economics: *n.* study of the application of scarce means to a given end (L. Robbins), forced daily upon the notice of the heads and staffs of English schools

economies of scale: *n.pl.*   fall in the average cost of something as more of it is produced: unknown in education, but its artificial pursuit led to the closure of village schools, the amalgamation of schools on widely separated sites and the creation of unwieldy establishments for as many as 2000 children

economy: *n.*   the third cliché of auditors (the other two are efficiency and effectiveness), indistinguishable in education from penury

editor: *n.*   person in charge of the content of a publication: editors are of two kinds, those who will publish a contribution they think good, whether they agree with it or not, and those who require every contribution to be what they might have written themselves; and the first of these is rare

educable: *adj.*   ready to endure at least eleven years of schooling and meet at least some of its requirements

educate: *v.*   so to treat children or others that they become or do what they could never otherwise have dreamt possible: the widespread misapprehension that 'educate' comes from the Latin *educere* and that it thus means a drawing out, whereas it patently comes from *educare*, to rear, bring up or nourish, has led to much weak sentimentality in schools, which has in turn attracted the scorn of the hardheaded

educated: *adj.*   systematically misled

education: *n.*   (i) the casting of false pearls before real swine (trad.)
(ii) that which discloses to the wise and disguises from the foolish their lack of understanding (A. Bierce)

(iii) originally the process of instruction but now its systematic organization in such a way as to inhibit learning and destroy talent

(iv) that which would enable people to spot a charlatan at forty paces were it not controlled by such people

educational experience: *n.*   (i) that which some teachers say that they arrange for pupils, to which no definite meaning can be attached

(ii) any experience except that of, or leading to, learning something

educationist: *n.*   one who cares, not about teaching, still less about learning, but about education: an additional syllable produces educationalist without adding anything to meaning

educator: *n.*   one who colludes in a nation's arrangements for the stultification of its children

effectiveness: *n.*   the second of the clichés of auditors (see efficiency and economy): capable of producing a desired result, unusual in formal education which produces results all right but seldom those desired

efficiency: *n.*   the first of the three clichés of auditors (the others are effectiveness and economy): the art of doing better more cheaply, constantly practised in schools and never in bureaucracies

eleven plus: *n.*   tests once given to ten-year-olds (that is, at eleven minus) to decide which should go to grammar and which to secondary modern schools: the subversive idea that children are not all the same was met with the claim that they are of just two kinds

élite: *n.* the choicest members of any group or society, often self-chosen, just to be sure: in a democracy élites are held in contempt until people want something important to themselves, when they do not go out of their way to find, for example, a non-élite heart surgeon

élitism: *n.* (i) pride in being, as one thinks, a member of an élite
(ii) belief that élites should be privileged and should be in charge
(iii) conspiracy attributed to those in desirable circumstances to explain the exclusion of oneself and others: making a charge of élitism in others is usually a claim to inferiority

ellipsis: *n.* ...

embus: *v.* load a coach with a school party going on a field trip, cultural excursion or foreign visit: the only feature of such a jaunt of which parents will have any reliable knowledge

emeritus: *adj.* superannuated: according to S. Leacock the phrase is made up of two Latin words meaning 'out' and 'because he deserved it'

encyclopaedia: *n.* (i) all there is to be known about everything, sometimes in one volume and sometimes in several
(ii) the quickest way to the pocket of an insecure and gullible parent

endemic: *adj.* prevalent in a specific group, like deference in teachers

engineering: *n.* getting from one state of affairs to another, as from one side of a river to another or from bread to toast (E. Krick)

England: *pr.n.* a country in which 'education produces no effect whatsoever' (O. Wilde): he added that if it did it would prove a serious danger to the upper classes and probably lead to acts of violence in Grosvenor Square, a thought that was remarkably prescient socially and geographically

English: *n.* (i) language unknown to officials and largely disappearing elsewhere

(ii) school subject designed to reveal the structure of the language (obs.): neither its presence nor its absence in schools seems to affect the tendency of the populace to muddle along with neither grammar nor syntax

(iii) school subject designed to reduce the attraction of great literature, thus minimizing the risk of intellectual and emotional development in the young

entitlement: *n.* the right to have something, in education usually a particular curriculum: unhappily the only way administrators can conceive of it is to make it compulsory, thereby turning a benefit into a burden

entrance: *n.* an exit from the outside, which is why securing university entrance stops one feeling an outsider

entrepreneur: *n.* the peak of human development, to be emulated by school children, unless he happens to be in jail

ephemeral: *adj.* short-lived, a quality shared by mayflies and Government wheezes

epidemiology: *n.* study of the development, spread, growth or treatment of pathological conditions, as in R. Dore's 'The Diploma Disease'

epistemology: *n.* (i) study of the grounds, limits and validity of knowledge, characterized in the past by the quest for certainty, through either authority or induction, though this is now thought to be mistaken: in knowledge certainty turns out to be less satisfactory than the possibility of progress

(ii) put briefly, knowing about knowing or, since nothing is certain, theories about theories

equality: *n.* political aspiration for equal interest in and treatment by the state, for example under the law: those who wish to prevent this seek to confuse the issue by pretending it implies the levelling of persons

error: *n.* mistake, false belief or wrong judgement, fruitful when discovered because this can provoke amendment and thus learning: in formal education it is commonly met with penalties, as if there were a tax on learning known as pain as you err

essay: *n.* written composition produced for the sole purpose of securing a mark or a grade

ET: *n.* educational technology; mechanical or electronic devices which may or may not be educational, depending on the desire, sense and skill of the learner

ethics: *n.* (i) that part of a code of practice that is not wholly self-serving

(ii) academic study of right conduct mercifully detached from actual behaviour

(iii) that which determines what is good and bad in the conduct of one's own life, as contrasted with morality which includes one's behaviour towards others and is thus more amenable to criticism

ethnic minority: *n.*   group of people who need constantly to be reminded that they are outsiders but in the nicest possible way (see euphemism)

etymology: *n.*   account of where words come from, suggestive if less important than noticing, in offical utterances, where words are going to

eunomia: *n.*   Greek for good government: the word does not exist in English, there being too little occasion to use it here

euphemism: *n.*   unreliable weapon in the battle between sentimentality and prejudice: thinking to improve an unfortunate situation by finding a kindlier word for it, the well-meaning discover instead that the new word itself has become offensive and hurtful, as when dunce was replaced by backward, then educationally subnormal and now special needs

euphuism: *n.*   affected speech, the preferred mode of a Prime Minister sermonizing about education

evaluation: *n.*   strictly, to judge the worth of: in education, to see whether people have done what they were told or what they themselves have promised, whether of value or not

evidence-based: *adj.*   of policy or practice said to be compatible with that research which confirms someone's prejudice

evil: *n.*   part-personalized force for great harm or wrong, present under more or less control in all human beings, who make evil as spiders make webs: progressive educators tend to think that, if they ignore it, it will go away, traditionalists that the least concession to individualism will release an epidemic of it

examination : *n.*   (i) an ordeal in which perhaps two years' conscientious toil and two hours' mugging up the night before garner the same reward, Grade B
   (ii) a rite in which those who do not wish to know ask questions of those who cannot tell (Sir W. Raleigh)
   (iii) an obstacle of which it is rational to be wary, since the greatest fool may ask more than a wise man may answer (C. Colton)
   (iv) an incentive to memorize without learning

examine: *v.*   generally to look at, scrutinize or investigate; in medicine to study all or part of a patient to see if he is ill; in law to interrogate formally, with a view to confirming or discrediting what someone says; in education to test whether someone has remembered what he has read or been told or can do what he has been shown: Socrates said that the unexamined life was not worth living but he was not thought to have had SATs in mind

examiner: *n.*   person whose relation to knowledge, truth and beauty was captured in the Punch cartoon of 1908, where two of them are walking in a wood: 'First examiner, "O cuckoo, shall I call thee bird, / Or but a wandering voice?" Second examiner, "State the alternative preferred, / With reasons for your choice"'

example: *n.*   (i) someone punished to encourage others

(ii) thing set, which may be either good or bad: the righteous, who set the former kind, are so abashed by their lack of following that they attribute irresistibility to the latter and denounce it, thus increasing its attraction

excellence: *n.*   (i) extreme goodness, specifically pursued by universities though there is no known means of judging whether it has been attained

(ii) a condition immediately recognizable by academics as characteristic of themselves

exceptional: *adj.*   admirably abnormal

exclamation mark: *n.*   popular punctuation mark, shunned by those who can read and write

exclusion: *n.*   (i) expulsion (see euphemism)

(ii) act of excluding, state of being excluded: a device for transferring the difficulties of one school to another, used only by good schools, never by bad

exercise book: *n.*   pupil's notebook: its name derives from a traditional educational method relying on mere repetition, pointless exertion and activity without progress, the mental equivalent of the exercise bike

exhibition: *n.*   clever and informative public display to which children are taken to be bored to death

experience: *n.*   thought substitute: when the young Karl Popper went to his teacher, Alfred Adler, with a question about a patient, Adler confidently offered diagnosis and solution, even though he did not know the patient, claiming to do so from his 'thousand-fold experience'; Popper retorted, 'And I suppose this makes the thousand-and-one-fold'

explanation: *n.* a careful and detailed account of an operation, structure or circumstance, guaranteed to confuse

extra-curricular: *adj.* of the education that becomes possible when schooling is temporarily suspended

extramural: *adj.* of classes patronizingly put on by universities for people they would not dream of admitting, provided the people keep well away

facetious: *adj.* one of the few English words with all the vowels in alphabetical order

fact: *n.* theory, hitherto unrefuted, that something is so

factory: *n.* Government-preferred model for educational institutions

faculty: *n.* plaything of university administrators, since the departments that compose it can be put together, taken apart, shuffled and redealt, and it can itself be renamed or turned into a 'school', none of this to any productive purpose

fad: *n.* intense but fleeting fashion, an essential component of any national directive, especially one produced on the advice of a committee (or see management guru)

fail: *v.* (i) avoid the approval of instructors, examiners and inspectors

(ii) gain too few marks in an examination to be awarded a qualification

failing schools: *part.*   what Secretaries of State and their Department have been doing for two decades

failure: *n.*   the inevitable but unintended consequence of every human endeavour, through which, happily, we learn: 'We have not failed: we have just found another way that doesn't work' (balloonist who ditched in the Pacific Ocean)

faith schools: *n.pl.*   (i) educational apartheid piously expressed
    (ii) generalization of a Prime Minister's prejudice

fallacy: *n.*   error, flawed argument, as in 'The girls who frequent picture palaces / Don't go in for psychoanalysis, / And although Dr Freud / May get very annoyed / They cling to their long-standing fallacies' (anon.)

fast track: *n.*   accelerated personal advancement, offered as a substitute for a desirable life

fax: *n.*   telephonic method of transmitting immediately that which rarely needs to be transmitted at all; the overuse of this device is known as faxual harassment

February: *n.*   low point of the academic year, requiring a half-term break or 'reading week' to conserve sanity

fee-paying: *ger.*   educative activity of parents, requiring forethought and sacrifice, to induce their offspring to regard their own lot with satisfaction and that of others with scorn

feedback: *n.*   excruciating noise produced when the output of a sound system leaks back into the input, hence metaphorically the response of one person, usually in authority, to the practice or presentation of another

fellowship: *n.*   membership of the governing body of a college, entailing the privilege of living well among enemies

feminism: *n.*   (i) unpleasantly assertive movement by women provoked by an unpleasantly assertive tendency in men: it has two main forms, the first demanding equal treatment with men in and from social institutions, the second claiming for women qualities, standards, values and capabilities preferable to those of men, and thus requiring not equality but privilege

(ii) a discriminatory theory which, in education, holds that girls are (a) the same as, or (b) different from boys and should thus be treated either the same or differently

fetish: *n.*   any object to which magical powers are attributed or excessive devotion offered, like statistics for an official

feudal: *adj.*   of a system of political, social, legal, economic and military relationships based on land tenure, now used as a term of mindless abuse against authority, wealth and privilege

fib: *n.*   a trivial and harmless lie: the precise degree of triviality and harmlessness is an important study among officials, since they would not wish to be caught in straightforward lying

fieldwork: *n.*   academic investigation done elsewhere than on the campus

figleaf: *n.*   element of sculpture that affects to conceal but in fact replaces a vital part, hence metaphorically a politician's justification for a policy

finance officer: *n.*   administrative officer appointed to keep the accounts of a university or college who by this means comes to control the funds, denying them to or withdrawing them from any academic activity which is unique, successful or admired in order to increase the staff of the finance office

finishing school: *n.*   private school, usually for girls, claiming to prepare them for an imagined adult life by teaching acceptable behaviour and accomplishments, indistinguishable in this respect from any other school

first degree: *n.*   award made by a university or college on the basis of three or four years' local residence, a certain quantity of writing which reproduces what the student has read or been told and a certificate to show that library books have been properly returned

flag: *n.*   designer textile once respected in education and society but now used chiefly for underwear and casual shirts

flattery: *n.*   insincere praise, being a proper attitude to superiors, since sincere praise is seldom possible, and the quickest way to get them to do what you want: should it prove ineffective, praise the resistance to it

flexible: *adj.*   unprincipled

floccinaucinilipilification: *n.*   making too much of underestimating

flogging: *ger.*   method of education once thought essential but for the present unfashionable and hence illegal

focus group: *n.*   substitute for political acumen, principle and purpose, fulfilling the function of the mob of more robust times

folklore: *n.*   the intellectual basis of formal educational practice

form: *n.*   the chief and devastating weapon of a bureaucracy: since nothing of importance can be accommodated on a form, its completion saps energy, intelligence and self-confidence, and time thus spent is at best wholly wasted

formal: *adj.*   in education, institutional, organized by rule and convention, a solution that has become a problem

foundation subject: *n.*   history, geography, music or PE in primary schools, synonymous with frills to the hard headed

fraction: *n.*   part of a whole, expressed by two numbers, one above and one below a line, the former, the numerator, showing how many there are of the latter, the denominator, being one of a number of equal parts into which the whole is divided: fractions in the plural are a school subject, presented as the manipulation of examples, so that most people are frightened when faced by three-quarters of four-fifths, when the reality is banal

France: *pr.n.* a barbarous and servile country in which Ministers of Education know every hour what every child is doing in school, as opposed to free and humane England where Secretaries of State know what every child is doing every quarter of an hour, or think they do

free school: *n.* one in which the inmates, though in custody, have some responsibility for themselves and the institution

free school meals: *n.pl.* practice introduced to prevent poor children going hungry and now maintained as yet another means of categorizing schools

French lesson: *n.* (i) period in a school timetable which inhibits the learning of French
    (ii) activity advertised in telephone boxes in which again little French is learned

Freudian: *adj.* relating to the work of an early twentieth-century fabulist: this is still taken seriously in university departments of English and Cultural Studies but nowhere else, least of all in psychology

Freudian psychology: *n.* (i) a gratuitous rigmarole
    (ii) an astonishingly imaginative construction offering insight into human behaviour: there are no grounds for preferring this definition to (i) above

frills: *n.pl.* any school activity which children enjoy or is valuable for some other reason, subject to periodic attack in favour of the 'basics'

frippery: *n.* academic dress

fun: *n.* one of the few things worth being serious about

fun and games: *n.pl.*   two things that never go together

futurism: *n.*   movement in literature and the arts beginning at the same time as modernism but now seen to have had less of a future

game: *n.*   (i) sport, pastime, amusement, once thought to build character now seen only to reveal it

(ii) diversion conducted according to rules, but not so grim as sport: the concept of 'playing the game' suggests that there is morality in it as well, but both are neglected when anything extraneous depends on the outcome of the game, like prestige or money.

GCSE: *n.*   General Certificate of Secondary Education, the latest doomed attempt to devise an examination for all school leavers aged 16 which does justice to individual achievements and means anything in itself: evidence for its inaptness lies in the constant tinkering to which it is subject

gender: *n.*   synonym for sex among the incurably confused

genes: *n.pl.*   that which makes it possible to make something of oneself, invented in 1911 by W. Johannson

genetics: *n.*   study of hereditability, which seems to have fewer implications for education the more successful it becomes

gentleman: *n.*   that which it was once the agreed object of education to produce: this has now been abandoned without another agreed object's having taken its place

geography: *n.*   school subject 'about maps, while history is about chaps' (trad.)

geometry: *n.*   algebra in pictures

Germany: *pr.n.*   a country with traditionally the most advanced and efficient system of education and the highest educational standards, where the populace were taken in by Hitler

gestalt psychology: *n.*   theories suggesting that learning takes place by developing 'insights', that is, by rearranging one's ideas of oneself and one's environment so as to make them of more use: the temptation in schools to change children's ideas for them simply misses the point

gibberish: *n.*   the language of official documents

gifted: *n.*   clever, talented, requiring sycophantic attention: the fact is that if an educational system will not do for the gifted it will not do for anyone else either

girl: *n.*   (i) female child, on average ahead of a male child physically, mentally, emotionally and socially, by way of compensation for the determination of most societies to put her behind as an adult
(ii) woman: the term is used thus by women in fun and friendship and by oafs who mistrust their own sense of superiority

glossary: *n.*   alphabetical list of terms with definitions or explanations, usually relating to a specialist field or subject and thus requiring another glossary to understand the definitions

good: *adj.*   vacuous and patronizing commendation by an ungenerous assessor, inspector or teacher

good school: *n.*   school which rejects bad pupils, but remember, 'You can't expect a boy to be vicious until he's been to a good school' ('Saki' – H. H. Munroe)

governors: *n.pl.*   unpaid persons with onerous statutory powers and duties in the management of schools, which they are willing to shoulder only because they do not know what these are

gown: *n.*   the traditional black robe of a university graduate once worn by teachers in secondary schools: since teachers stopped cleaning the blackboard with its long sleeves, standards have fallen dreadfully

grade: *n.*   a rating of achievement in education, lacking the spurious precision of a mark or the helpfulness of a judgement

graduate: *n.*   one who has tricked a university or college into awarding him a first degree: the cachet attached to this is less now than it was because so many more people have learnt how the trick is worked

graffiti: *n.pl.*   reliable indicators of the morale of a school, particularly those in the girls' lavatories

grammar: *n.*   means of showing the relation between words in a language, prolonged study of which is unconvincingly asserted to lead to clarity of expression

grammar school: *n.*   school which carefully selects children as being most apt for its purpose and still fails a quarter of them

grant-maintained school: *n.*   school that once became so impatient with its dependence on a local authority that it allowed itself to be bribed into servitude to the Secretary of State

graph: *n.*   statistics in pictures

gravity: *n.*   (i) the attraction of one body for another (ii) a repellent cloak for the vapidity of official utterance

Greek: *n.*   the language of the foundations of Western art, science, philosophy and politics, revived in the Renaissance, revered by the Victorians, and hence negligible in modern education

green paper: *n.*   once a pamphlet, so called from the colour of its cover, setting out Government proposals for discussion and improvement, now a glossy magazine, illustrated by pictures of the Prime Minister, comprising unsubstantiated assertions, begged questions, half-baked proposals and scarcely-veiled threats, followed by a questionnaire rigged to show support

group: *n.*   number of persons considered as a single unit, encouraging the study of interactions within groups (group dynamics) and the treatment of individuals through membership of a group (group therapy): no unequivocal benefits are known from these proceedings, and some visible harm

GTC: *n.*   General Teaching Council, a welcome intrusion of self-regulation into the profession of teaching, flawed by the dominance of the Secretary of State, the conflict of interest involved in union representation and an itch in the Council itself to meddle in what does not properly concern it, like research and representation

guidance: *n.*   (i) counsellors' name for advice, equally unacceptable
(ii) third category of communication from the DfES, telling people how to do what the DfES has decided so as to make it work (see circular)

gymnasium: *n.*   (i) grammar school in German
(ii) large, airless room with wallbars at the windows and stocked with vaulting horses and other instruments of torture

habit: *n.*   settled tendency or practice: habits are of two kinds; good, which are established with effort and constant schooling, and bad, which are picked up in a trice and require effort and constant schooling to eradicate

half term: *n.*   week-long break in the middle of a school term to preserve the sanity of pupils and teachers

haver: *v.*   in Scotland to blather, in England to dither: as a local education authority in London shows, it is possible to combine these meanings

he, him (acc), his (gen): *pron.* brief word causing endless difficulty to those who cannot distinguish sex from grammar: 'he' stands for 'he or she', whereas 'she' stands for 'she' alone, and supposing or insisting otherwise leads to the collapse of syntax and the death of style, as in 'the student, looking over his or her shoulder . . .' (R. Barnett)

head of year: *n.* a post of 'responsibility' carrying no necessary duties and an extra pittance

headteacher: *n.* a person combining the responsibilities of managing director, finance officer, psychologist, psychiatrist, prison governor, lawyer and impresario, and thus paid less than any of these

heaven: *n.* place to which those favoured by a god or gods go to live in everlasting bliss: by tradition the gods favour the heroic and the persecuted, so those who cannot abide classroom teachers should avoid heaven

hell: *n.* place of eternal pain and punishment after death with special accommodation (after Dante) for those who had power in life and so tried to produce these conditions for others without their having to die first

heredity: *n.* that which enables us to become what we are: the idea that it therefore determines what we are is as fallacious as all determinism

heresy: *n.* next year's orthodoxy

heuristic: *adj.* by discovery (for Archimedes, discovery by bathing): a method of learning that should imply rigour and method but has come, in the hands of the sentimental, to mean messing about

heuristics: *n.*   problem solving without logic (cf. algorithm)

hiccups: *n.*   a diaphragmatic spasm: in the singular, a hiccup is a fatal flaw in a cherished proposal of which its authors wish to make light, as when the scheme of performace-related pay was found to be illegal

hierarchy: *n.*   graded ranks in a government by a priesthood, a form of organization unfit for any other purpose

highbrow: *n.*   derisive term used by lowbrows (q.v.) for those of scholarly, erudite or cultivated tastes

hindsight: *n.*   (i) wisdom-substitute for the smug, often in the form of scorn for the neglect at the time of considerations that could be known only later
   (ii) term of abuse for the rational criticism of an earlier blunder
   (iii) perfect vision

history: *n.*   (i) what you can remember (W. C. Sellar and R. J. Yeatman)
   (ii) an account mostly false, of events mostly unimportant which are brought about by rulers mostly knaves and soldiers mostly fools (A. Bierce) and thus especially edifying for children (cf. geography)

holiday: *n.*   school version of vacation, derived from Old English for holy day, distinguished from the unholy days of term

home: *n.*   (i) source of whatever it is that makes it hard for a child to be taught in formal education
   (ii) place where children are expected to learn what someone has failed to teach them in school

homework: *n.*   (i) school work not done at home

(ii) futile attempt to compensate for what has not been mastered under instruction and supervision by demanding further work uninstructed and unsupervised

(iii) schoolwork done by parents

homoerotic: *adj.*   inducing sexual feelings in a member of the same sex, leading to a common enough experience which right-minded persons deny in themselves and excoriate in others

homosexuality: *n.*   (i) sexual attraction which, according to law, may be promoted by schools so long as this is not at the behest of a local authority

(ii) the only topic thought by a significant number of people to be offensive or harmful on which there is a legal inhibition as regards schools (see above) which a significant number of people consider offensive and harmful but which is compulsory

honours list: *n.*   sytem of national rewards which incorporates its own punishment: any possible pleasure at receiving an honour must evaporate on reading the rest of the list

human capital: *n.*   labour

humane: *adj.*   kindly, empathetic: formal education can be said to be humane in the same sense as a humane killer, in that it anaesthetizes the victims and makes the onlookers feel better

humanities: *n.pl.*   formerly contrasted with theology (the goddities?) and consisting of the 'polite studies', sc. Greek and Roman history, literature and philosophy;

these things having been neglected, the term is applied to almost anything outside the physical and social sciences

hyphen: *n.*   equivocal punctuation mark which seems to link but rather serves to keep apart (J. Brody), as in Asian-British

hypnopaedia: *n.*   the learning of lessons during sleep, explaining why lectures are not wholly ineffective

hypocrisy: *n.*   (i) morality's first line of defence
   (ii) quality popularly attributed to politicians, but few of them have the moral development to make hypocrisy possible

hypothalamus: *n.*   the seat of sin, as identified by medical science

hypothesis: *n.*   a hunch: the thing to do with a hypothesis is to test it and to maintain it only so long as it survives the tests or until a better one comes along, otherwise it will turn into a fallacy and be much more difficult to give up

hypothetical: *adj.*   of the nature of a hypothesis, sc. provisional, conjectural but testable, now vulgarized to mean merely imaginary or conditional, as in hypothetical situation: a hypothetical question is one that a politician wishes had not been asked

hysteria: *n.*   uncontrolled emotional state of fear, anger or excitement, induced in schools by a visit from OFSTED, deliberately used by the Secretary of State as an instrument of control

hysterical: *adj.*   literally 'of the womb', thus used of a frenzied emotional reaction to a minor upset, a characteristic of male-dominated organizations

idea: *n.*   flight of fancy, result of thought, product of reflection, proposal for action, a candidate for euthanasia in any institution because of the terror it induces in the staff, especially senior ones

ideal: *n.*   unattainable perfection for which moralists would nevertheless have us strive, lest we fall into torpor: happiness more reliably follows imperfect but attainable improvement

ideology: *n.*   a ritual system whose power increases with its obscurity and inapplicability

idioglossia: *n.*   private language invented by children, or by the DfES to describe its futile endeavours

idleness: *n.*   reprehensible consequence of freedom: as OFSTED made clear in its 1999 report on Summerhill School, if a free person should choose to be idle, freedom must be abolished

ignoramus: *n.*   one who not only does not know but, worse, knows what is not so, a condition whose enhancement is the chief purpose of the mass media

ignorance: *n.*   (i) that which A does not know and B does, enabling B to sneer: since our ignorance is boundless, that portion of it singled out for scorn changes constantly, from the second law of thermodynamics (late 1950s) to phoneme (late 1990s)

(ii) an evil which formal education is wrongly thought to remedy, which is a pity since people who know nothing can be told anything

(iii) that quality in a politician which renders him invincible

(iv) pitfall of a lexicographer, leading even the great S. Johnson to define pastern as the knee of a horse

illiteracy: *n.* condition of a constant proportion of any population, fluctuating numbers of whom can read and write

illiterate: *adj.* qualified for television journalism

imagination: *n.* creative ability, resourcefulness, sympathy; welcome in institutions only if heavily disguised as procedure

impart: *v.* relate or bestow: one of the many words in education which implies without justification that what has been offered has been received, prompting the overconfident error that improving the delivery will guarantee reception

imposition: *n.* (i) a punishment for pupils, such as the writing of lines (obs.)

(ii) a punishment for teachers, such as the writing of returns and reports

(iii) a favoured *modus operandi* of the Secretary of State

improve: *v.* take action alleged to benefit the lot of others which inexplicably attracts their opprobrium and resistance

inclusion: *n.*   name given to a policy under which it is forbidden to send home a child who has headlice

incompetence: *n.*   the mother of ambition

inculcate: *v.*   compel assent or acceptance by insistent repetition, as a hammer inculcates a nail into a plank

independence: *n.*   capable autonomy and the mastery of circumstance, a stated object of formal education and its most usual victim

independent school: *n.*   school which voluntarily embraces most of the crass values, curricular rigidities and meaningless assessments which the Government forces on others

independent study: *n.*   the responsible planning by a student of a programme of study and the pursuit of this to a recognizably successful conclusion, requiring dedicated time for the student to think and plan, a serious requirement for private study, individual tutorial arrangements, access to specialist tuition, assurance of the validity of the students' programmes and of the probity of their assessment: all this is asserted to be both impossible and needing constant vigilance in its prevention

individual: *n.*   the only entity capable of learning, posing a problem for formal education which takes place in groups: teachers solve this problem by maximizing individual attention, officials by eliminating individuality

individualism: *n.*   doctrine requiring the strictest controls against its infection of children and teachers

indoctrinate: *v.* secure, by force or guile, uncritical assent to some system of belief which calm reflection would reject

industry: *n.* (i) diligence, assiduity; an academic virtue on which a reputation may be based

(ii) source of funds newly discovered by some academics, on whose success in tapping it, reputations may be based

inertia: *n.* powerful force in human and social affairs, to be overcome only from within

infant: *n.* child whose chief task and joy is to prepare for key stage 1

infidel: *n.* Christian, Muslim or gentile

inform: *v.* tell or reveal: when the benefactors who do this notice the apathy of their listeners they leap to the erroneous conclusion that they should inform more and more energetically

information: *n.* (i) whatever one has been told: given the prevalence of information, it is suggestive that so little is known (cf. knowledge)

(ii) that which is potentially usable by someone informing himself or by someone wishing to inform others, of which the first of these is by far the more promising: people speak of information being available but without conscious persons, information is inert

(iii) anything that the DfES is at present proposing (see circular)

information technology: *n.* (i) the electronics used to produce babel

(ii) those devices which make it possible for people to inform themselves: people talk of the storage, retrieval and transfer of information, but it is only bits which are stored and so on, and these become information only when consciously sought

initiative: *n.*   casual and capricious meddling, a substitute for the systematic energy of effective reform

innate: *adj.*   inborn, a description of abilities inherent in individuals which formal education is not organized to discover: most of the innate abilities that it does recognize and seek to develop are limited and crass, the exception being language which it systematically mistreats

innocent: *adj.*   ingenuous or blameless, a condition much less common than the sentimental think, even at the earliest ages

innovator: *n.*   one who does something new himself, as distinct from a reformer, who does something new to others, and a radical, who does to others something that is old enough to have been forgotten: innovation carries an automatic penalty, cf. 'Never be a pioneer. It's the Early Christian that gets the fattest lion' ('Saki' – H. H. Munroe)

INSET: *n.*   (i) in-service education and training, something inserted into the professional life of teachers and having little relation to the problems encountered in their classrooms or other school activities

(ii) opportunity for teachers to show off to adults rather than to children

INSET day: *n.*   whole day devoted by the staff of a school to the demands of external bodies and the neglect of the children and institutions in their charge: such a day can be productive only if organized as a party

inspect: *v.*   once, to observe, reflect and report on schools and other institutions so as to enhance understanding of the nature and state of education; now to examine for compliance with external requirements

inspection: *n.*   (i) official scrutiny of an activity or institution, best done by asking what is being done, whether this is worth doing and whether it is being done well, but now merely a checking of items against a list so as to be smugly censorious about the inevitable mismatches
   (ii) the only activity of the misnamed Office for Standards in Education: without the bullying bluster of the first chief inspector, OFSTED is revealed as having no thought-out principles or worked-out practice of inspection

inspector: *n.*   once, a person who, after observing schools and reflecting on what he saw, reported to the Secretary of State on the general condition of education and to the individual schools on their strengths and weaknesses; now a poor drudge who checks the performance of a school against a predetermined set of criteria in order that the Secretary of State may sneer about the school and vilify teachers generally

institute: *n.*   society for the promotion of some object, usually the interests of its members

institute of education: *n.*   part of a university devoted to the instruction of graduates wishing to teach, on the mistaken assumption that graduates are educated

institution: *n.* (i) organization founded for a purpose, now forgotten, and thus devoted to quite different and incompatible purposes, including the comfort of its staff

institutional ignorance: *n.* that particularly virulent kind of ignorance created in institutions, usually Governmental, whose organization, operation and power effectively preclude learning

instruct: *v.* direct or command, hence teach or demonstrate peremptorily

instruction: *n.* a pedagogical practice without known justification: 'If you tell me I shall forget; if you show me I shall remember; if I do it I shall understand' (anon.) but this overestimates the value of showing

instructions: *n.pl.* (i) directions on how to do something, usually accompanying a form, device or implement, incomprehensible to anyone who does not already know how to do it, in which it has much in common with instruction in the singular

(ii) to an advanced anthropomorphist, the operation of DNA or the set of bits specifying a computer operation and the data on which it rests

instructor: *n.* one who stultifies by explanation

insubordination: *n.* kicking against the pricks

insulting: *adj.* of the quality of most official guidance to teachers

intellectual: *n.* (i) foreign person, usually French, much given to pretentious nonsense

(ii) in England, however, 'To the man in the street who, I'm sorry to say, / Is a keen observer of life, / The word "Intellectual" suggests straight away / A man who's untrue to his wife.' (W. H. Auden)

(iii) one educated beyond the bounds of common sense (P. Marples)

intelligence: *n.*   (i) mental capacity, that which enables one to understand how little of it one has

(ii) information: this use is chiefly military, but officials too find that it is easier to use than (i) above

(iii) that which is measured by intelligence tests (trad.)

intelligence test: *n.*   set of procedures bearing a more than superficial resemblance to jigsaw and crossword puzzles, which for more than a century have been used to diagnose intellectual ability, having uses and consequences both benign and malign: on the bright side, the tests may persuade teachers to wonder whether a child's doing badly at school may derive from something other than stupidity and the child himself to suspect that he might not be as daft as he had consistently been told; on the dark side they have been perverted to the bureaucratic purpose of allocating children to different kinds of schools (though even here they are less vulnerable than other methods to manipulation by the privileged) and equally perversely they may so emphasize ability as to persuade some teachers and children that little is to be gained from disciplined effort

intelligent: *adj.*   being able to hold opposing ideas in mind at the same time, enjoying it and not being paralysed

intelligentsia: *n.*   (i) those in a society who are vastly more educated, cultivated and intellectual than anyone else: in England there are no such persons, so the term has never caught on

intentions: *n.pl.*   the stated aims of Government: always good, they lead straight to Hell for others

internet: *n.*   (i) a means of fast access to worldwide information, bearing the same relation to education as fast food to gastronomy
   (ii) device whereby persons unknown, seeking power, profit or self-gratification, are able to manipulate children free from the intervention of parents or teachers (D. Ravitch)

interview: *n.*   the best-known method for appointing to any post the least suitable of the available candidates

investment: *n.*   spending on education and other public services

invigilator: *n.*   policemen whose beat is an examination room

IQ: *n.*   intelligence quotient, discovered by dividing mental age (derived from tests) by chronological age (derived from a birth certificate) and multiplying the result by a hundred, a proceeding that has neither justification nor point: its meaninglessnes is revealed when one considers that IQ in all countries is increasing by an average of three points in a decade, without their populations' becoming noticeably more intelligent

Islam: *n.*   the latest religion to demand educational privilege at public expense, but unlikely to catch up with Christianity in this respect

itch: *n.*   an affliction of Secretaries of State which impels them to interfere in matters which they do not understand

jargon: *n.*   language used by specialists and others to conceal their meaning

job enrichment: *n.*   making tasks less routine by increasing personal responsibility and satisfaction, and hence morale: in education those who claim to have the same object reverse the process

judgement: *n.*   a quality whose absence in all educational and psychological tests and measures is of the essence

junior: *n.*   child who has done with key stage 1 and is now agog for key stage 2

justice: *n.*   a nonentity: 'there is no justice' is a truth well known to pupils, students, teachers and parents alike

Kafkaesque: *adj.*   creating a nightmarish sense of helplessness against a sinister and impersonal bureaucracy with an over-riding mad logic of its own, characteristic of educational administration since 1988

key stage: *n.*   barbarously mixed metaphor for a critical time which reveals that those governing education are illiterate and conceals the fact that the time concerned is not critical but arbitrary

kindergarten: *n.*   foreign nursery school taking children of an age at which in England they are relentlessly taught and tested: needless to say, it is the foreigners who seem to benefit more from their later education

knowledge: *n.*   that in oneself which in others is merely opinion

laboratory: *n.*   school room furnished and equipped to mislead students as to the nature, purposes and methods of science

laconic: *adj.*   obsolete form of speech

Latin: *n.*   an international language of government, diplomacy, theology, history, science, philosophy and education for one and a-half millennia in the Western world, now dropped from the curriculum as dead and worthless

law of education: *n.*   in the olden days, the constitutional arrangements created by Parliament for the independent operation of schools and other educational institutions, and hence the book containing these; today, a set of detailed and rigid controls over the life and activity of pupils, students, teachers and the institutions in which they work, subject to annual or more frequent changes: five large loose-leaf albums are barely sufficient to encompass it

league tables: *n.pl.*   (i) attempt, so far unsuccessful, to intrude the ethics of football into education

(ii) lists indicating supposed failings among schools, issued to distract people from the real failings of the Secretary of State

learn: v. bring about a significant change in one's understanding and capability, in which memory, repetition, knowledge and skill may have been a help

learned journal: *n.*   publication which even its authors find hard to read

learner: *n.*   one who discovers something he does not know or cannot do and desires to remedy this, hence formulating the problem, proposing a solution and testing it: this is different from committing to memory or increasing facility, though these may well assist learning

learning: *n.*   that which people do if they can escape teaching, schooling and education

learning by heart: *ger.*   remembering with understanding and affection a piece of poetry or prose, the antithesis of learning by rote

learning curve: *n.*   graphical image of progress of learning over time, the steeper the curve the faster the learning: it is naïvely assumed that the graph always slopes upwards, but there is much evidence to the contrary, for example in the first year of secondary school

learning environment: *n.*   not an environment that learns, in contrast to learning organization, but a polysyllabic circumlocution for a school or classroom

learning support: *n.* employment of a separate teacher to help a child to make sense of another teacher's lesson, required to some extent by all children but usually restricted to those with a statement

learning theory: *n.* set of ideas, sometimes plausible, bizarre or discredited, about how learning takes place: the known theories are mutually inconsistent and even incompatible, and agree on one thing only, that learning depends on the initiative and activity of the learner, so formal education works on the opposite principle that it depends on the activity of teachers or, worse, the state

lecture: *n.* (i) a performance whereby the notes of the lecturer become the notes of the student without passing through the mind of either (trad.)

(ii) respite from academic or other work: a student tempted by another to cut a lecture argued, 'I cannot afford to miss it; I need the sleep'

(iii) a reproof whose force is in inverse proportion to its length

lecture room: *n.* dormitory theatre

lecturer: *n.* one who is paid to teach on the grounds that he was once able to learn (F. M. Cornford)

legislate: *v.* to bind others without thought

legislation: *n.* the making of new laws, a thirteenth-century innovation to which Governments have become incurably addicted; legislation now comes in two kinds, primary legislation in the form of bills which become acts after cursory debate in the House of Commons and sporadic scrutiny in the House of Lords, and secondary legislation in the form of statutory instruments treated by both Houses with insouciance: in education both kinds are multiplying beyond reason and control, prompting the DfES to produce, in addition, virtually endless official guidance

lesser evil: *n.*   course which few Secretaries of State can bring themselves to choose

liberal: *adj.*   generous or tolerant, once plausibly associated with a political movement, but with no contemporary party

liberal arts: *n.pl.*   in the middle ages, grammar, logic, rhetoric, arithmetic, geometry, music and astronomy: it is a measure of the advance of civilization that most of this has been excluded from the school curriculum and what remains is etiolated

librarian: *n.*   (i) one who holds, guards, classifies and arranges books so as to make them available to others: when librarians rise high in their profession they undergo a spontaneous change which leads them ruthlessly to destroy and dispose of the books in their charge

(ii) bookish person who, in the view of most politicians and officials, would be better occupied servicing computers and video machines, lest the populace, old and young, might lack distraction

library: *n.*   (i) room or building containing little but books, an imperfect defence against being overcome by information

(ii) compendium or series of books as in the Library of Valuable Knowledge, the opposite of which would be jolly, or the Library of Entertaining Knowledge, both of which are known to the lexicographer

life: *n.*   (i) the human condition: 'Such is life and all things show it; / We're all damn fools but we don't all know it' (remembered by A. E. Adams)

(ii) energy, liveliness, awareness, animation: a dangerous attribute which when found in schools it is the duty, pleasure and policy of officials to extirpate

(iii) a sexually transmitted disease for which education is an imperfect cure

lifelong learning: *n.*   (i) a statement of the obvious, since everyone does it, more or less

(ii) a worthy aspiration, though suggestions that it is being accommodated institutionally are false

(iii) infrequent bouts of training in obsolescent skills undertaken to secure the dole

literacy: *n.*   the ability to read and write, considered so important by officials (who do little else) that schools are forced to insist that those to whom it comes hard persist fruitlessly with it at the expense of all the things they could do easily and well

literally: *n.*   journalese for metaphorically or virtually, as in 'He literally wiped the floor with his opponent'

literate: *adj.*   able to read and write, with the seldom fulfilled expectation that the reading will be with understanding and the writing with sense

local education authority: *n.*   endangered species, rather more attractive than the predators that are after them

logic: *n.*   application of principles of thought and argument to the solution of problems, both practical and theoretical, to which emotion, intuition, bargaining, bullying and neglect are widely preferred

longitudinal study: *n.*   survey of a group of contemporary children as they grow up, spread over enough years to expunge the memory of its original purpose and producing recommendations for circumstances that no longer pertain

look and say: *adj.*   of a method of teaching the reading of English as if it were Chinese, by memorizing the shape of individual words or guessing the meaning from shape and context

lottery: *n.*   principle on which marks are awarded in an examination

lowbrow: *n.*   derisive term used by highbrows (q.v.) for those of uncultivated or unintellectual tastes

loyalty: *n.*   (i) the habit of heartfelt support: like many virtues it becomes evil if enforced
    (ii) 'always an evil' (B. Russell)

lucubration: *n.*   literally by lamplight, hence laborious study or its result in a conference paper

luxury: *n.*   a condition offering such dreadful temptations that Governments work day and night to keep it out of schools

maintained school: *n.*   an ill-maintained school

man of letters: *n.*   one who wrote articles, mainly critical, now extinct: there were no women of letters, since those women who wrote, wrote books

management: *n.*   unconvincing substitute for leadership

margin: *n.*   blank space down the side of a pupil's written work for a teacher's scholia, in the form of ticks, crosses, praise, insults and corrections

mark: *n.*   (i) the currency of pedagogues
(ii) name for a child at all key stages (P. Marples)

marketing: *ger.*   trying to sell something: teachers are often urged to sell themselves more effectively and should clearly consider on-the-job training in Soho and Shepherd Market

masochism: *n.*   useful interest for those working in modern education: you have to take your pleasures where you can

master: *n.*   ship with a specified number of masts: it is unclear how this relates to the name for a male teacher, though unlike mistress the word can be a verb indicating intellectual or physical control over something or someone

mathematics: *n.*   study made up of arithmetic, algebra, geometry and calculus (qq.v.), now superseded for practical purposes by computers, much as studying shadows was long ago superseded by watches, and thus reverting to its essence as a beautiful and fascinating intellectual diversion

media: *n.pl.*   contraction of mass media of communication, the means by which a nation's population gets to know anything: what children know by this means is ignored in formal curricula and syllabuses

medical students: *n.pl.*   traditionally, infantile pranksters, drunks and rugby players training for the sensitive and intelligent care of the sick and dying: today these make up about half the numbers, the remainder having less flaunted weaknesses

mediocre: *adj.*   deplorably ordinary

mediocrity: *n.*   state of education required by the Government, provided that they can find a way of awarding it higher marks each year

medium: *n.*   form, means or materials for executing a work of art or craft: the plural, media, is now used only an a contraction for mass media of communication, and pejoratively at that

meeting: *n.*   less effective substitute for remedial action than research (q.v.): it is always possible that at the end of a meeting someone will unequivocally be given something to do, with the promise of another meeting to see if he has done it

memorandum: *n.*   that which ought to be remembered, a gerundive: its form makes clear that whoever its ostensible recipient may be a memorandum is written chiefly for the benefit of its author

memory: *n.*   mental storage and recall of facts, feelings and thoughts: memory is an important aid to learning but not learning itself, and the failure to make this distinction has rendered much of formal education useless

mendicancy: *n.*   activity deplored by Government, except in educational institutions where it is encouraged

mental age: *n.*   ingenous and inconsequential idea of expressing a child's score in an intelligence test by the age at which the average child gets the same score, used in reading age

mental arithmetic: *n.*   the only branch of arithmetic of any use after leaving primary school, but most people prefer calculators

mental discipline: *n.*   theory of learning that assumes that mental power can be exercised and trained, usually by the teacher's being visibly cleverer than the students and adept at devising for them grindingly boring tasks: the fact is that a mind can be trained only by the person who owns it (P. Scott)

mentor: *n.*   tutor overseeing the whole programme of a pupil or advising a trainee on teaching practice, in both cases the object is to help to make sense of whatever other instruction is being given

merit: *n.*   quality in themselves to which the foolish attribute their good fortune

metaphor: *n.*   an implied simile, where one term of a comparison is substituted for the other; metaphors may be live, dead or mixed, live ones recalling the imagery of their origin and dead ones not: in educational speeches and policy-making metaphores are an infallible sign of vacuity and confusion, as in targets, key stages, benchmarks, beacons and the like

method: *n.*   (i) a way of doing something, a frequently observed component of madness (trad., after W. Shakespeare)
   (ii) that which gives mastery, more reliably than knowledge gives power

methodology: *n.*   the study, organization or development of method: the word is much used by the pretentious when all they mean is 'method'

middlebrow: *n.*   derisive term used by highbrows for those they regard as having conventional tastes or limited culture

militancy: *n.*   aggressive reaction, as of the tibialis anterior muscle when the tendon just below the patella is tapped

millennium: *n.*   a nine-days wonder

mind: *n.*   faculty of thought, often regarded as an immaterial part of a person: school and university courses assume that the mind is wholly immaterial

minded: *adj.*   condition of a politician contemplating a course of action which he is unwilling to take until he is sure that he can get away with it

minor: *n.*   child legally and officially deemed irresponsible and thus tempted to behave accordingly

miracle: *n.*   the survival of the human race in the face of all that formal educational systems have done for it

mission statement: *n.*   platitudinous substitute for knowing what to do and how to do it

missionary: *n.*   teacher who has a call to offer children and others abroad what is even less apt for them than for those left at home

mistake: *n.*   blunder or misconception, recognition of which is the beginning of learning: ridicule and punishment for mistakes are the chief reasons why so little is learnt

mistress: *n.*   a female teacher, any woman in authority or one living with a man: historically the first of these was chaste, the second chaste or married, the third neither, but these moral distinctions can no longer be relied on

modern languages: *n.pl.*   a study which after seven years' drudgery in school furnishes its devotees with less fluency than a fortnight in a foreign country with a good phrasebook

modernism: *n.*   (i) intellectual movement, chiefly in the arts and philosophy, at least 100 years old and still incoherent
(ii) in school architecture, the excuse for leaking roofs and porous walls

modernize: *v.*   (i) cause to look modern
(ii) to make unjustified and pointless changes usually based on a mixture of ideas discredited elsewhere or in other times, any half-formed notion that emerges in a focus group and a wheeze that occured late at night to a youth in a suit in Millbank Tower: any change that does not remedy an abuse or redress a grievance, or is not meant to, leads to more of both without compensating improvement

module: *n.*   basic unit of fitted kitchens and educational courses: in schools an attempt may be made to see that modules add up to a coherent course, in universities seldom, so that a modular course is the academic equivalent of day-tripping

money: *n.*   legal tender, with which one may buy goods and services, replaced in education by euphemisms: let it be recognized that English schools do not lack resources, means, facilities or provision; what they lack is money

monitor: *n.*   (i) primary school child with a little job to do: since free milk was abolished, the grandest of them, the milk monitor, has disappeared

(ii) person appointed to check and report on the actions of those more expert and responsible than himself

(iii) a lizard

monograph: *n.*   a treatise on a single, preferably obscure, subject, considered as if through a microscope

morpheme: *n.*   word or syllable carrying meaning, unlike phoneme, which carries no meaning on its own and is thus the offically preferred basis for learning to read

mortar board: *n.*   stiff cap with extended flat top and awkward tassle emblematic of graduation: photographs of wearers show that the oddity of the gear in no way diminishes their self-satisfaction

mortification: *n.*   reaction of teachers to the discredited theory and farcical practice of performance-related pay

motivation: *n.*   desire or incentive: the word derives from psychology, where it is empty of useful meaning, and it allows educators to assert the importance of motivation while discouraging the desire to learn and witholding incentives to do so

multicultural education: *n.*   instruction in racism masquerading as toleration

multiple choice question: *n.*   examination question in which the candidate is asked to choose between a number of given answers, thus shortening the odds on his giving a wrong one; academic version of the game of call-my-bluff

multiplication tables: *n.pl.*   systematically arranged series of results of multiplying two numbers together, convenient for chanting, like psalms in old-fashioned churches: reliance on them in later life testifies to a failure of mathematical education and understanding

mythology: *n.*   the history that most people remember, for example that the grammar schools were abolished by Shirley Williams, when most of the grammar schools that were abolished fell at the hand of Margaret Thatcher

naming and shaming: *ger.pl.*   arbitrary nomination of certain schools for the benefits of the pillory: having the predictable effect of demoralizing all other schools as well

National Curriculum: *pr.n.*   totalitarian attempt to control the lives of children by determining centrally what they should do at school: since no control is exercised over the controllers, their requirements change arbitrarily and annually, making it impossible for the public to know what damage is being done

needs: *n.pl.*   a socio-educational term of no discernible meaning and hence in constant use

neurosis: *n.*   dottiness beyond a joke

Newspeak: *pr.n.*   a language of oppression, shrunken and perverted so as to exclude unwanted ideas and assert the opposite of the truth (invented by G. Orwell): modern Governments more smoothly use lots of words but deprive them of any meaning whatever

night school: *n.*   institution in which students learn as much in a few hours a week as do those in day schools who have the leisure to attend full time

nightmare: *n.*   the conviction, in a teacher, that a politician may mean what he says

nits: *n.pl.*   one of the few things children indubitably gain from attendance at school

no: *sent. sub.*   expression of denial, disapproval, disbelief or refusal: the last of these is a recourse used defensively by the weak and aggressively by the inadequate

nonsense: *n.*   words or actions that make no sense, popularized by Edward Lear: 'They went to sea in a sieve, they did. / In a sieve they went to sea', and by the DfES: 'Unless you have crossed the new performance threshold you will be on the new pay spine'

not viable: *adj.*   a lie used of a good, popular and successful small school in order to facilitate its destruction

numeracy: *n.*   the ability to manipulate numbers: there are those who get fun out of this, but for most people it seems futile and tedious, and they can do it with success, satisfaction and profit only when the numbers relate to something in which they are passionately interested

numerate: *adj.*   able to use numbers, a neologism from the 1960s, formed by analogy with literate: neither word can aptly be applied to more than a handful of school leavers

nursery school: *n.*   a contradiction in terms, the first term implying an ethos and practice antithetical to that of the second

O level: *n.*   former examination for 16-year-olds now remembered fondly because the reasons for its replacement have been forgotten

objective: *n.*   metaphor whose military origin is rightly overlooked (see aim and aims and objectives)

objective test: *n.*   test that excludes judgement on the part of the person marking it

obsolete: *adj.*   of long standing and working well but vulnerable to attack from politicians believing they must do something

official: *adj.*   emanating from a Government department: 'Never believe anything until it has been officially denied' (A. E. Adams)

OFSTED: *pr.n.*   (i) Office for Standards in Education, which is not an office, without standards and nothing to do with education: remember, 'there is only one F in OFSTED' (anon.)

(ii) organization issuing reports which are the educational equivalent of station announcements, intrusive, vaguely menacing and unintelligible

old boy: *n.*   boy who has not noticed that he is now grown up and can give up his attachment to school or college

old boy network: *n.*   the means by which men ensure that the best jobs are taken by those stuck in the same pre-pubertial stage as themselves: that there is no old girl network is another example of the inherent inferiority of women

old girl: *n.*   member of a nearly extinct species, believing on the basis of her own education, normally in a girls' school, that women are capable of achievement

omniscience: *n.*   an attribute of God, in humans the nearest approximation is a knowall

only: *adj.* and *adv.*   unique: always misplaced in speech and writing, as in 'Passengers must only cross the line by the footbridge', rather, one supposes, than having a party on it or throwing themselves off

ontology: *n.*   the study of being or existence, distinguishable from any study of what is or exists

open book examination: *n.*   a remedy for the criticism that success in an examination requires little but simple recall, permitting the use of a crib and thus requiring little but copying

open day: *n.*   occasion for parents and public to visit a school during which much of interest is hidden away

Open University: *n.*   night school with added television

opinion: *n.*   (i) what someone thinks about something: it is the postmodernist fashion to assert that one opinion is as good as another, but this is merely to obviate the trouble of learning to distinguish

(ii) a boon inspiring universal generosity, since everyone wishes to give it and none to receive it: 'If you want my opinion . . .' / To someone I said, he / Replied with 'No, thank you, / I've got one already' (W. Plinge)

opinion poll: *n.*   method of persuading people to think, do or want what you require of them by pretending to ask them about it

opportunity: *n.*   chance: the longer word is to be preferred in educational discourse (a) because it is longer and (b) because the use of the shorter in phrases like 'equality of opportunity' would show them to be meaningless

opportunity cost: *n.*   that which you lose when by doing one thing you cannot do another, for example when a marginal increase in primary school maths scores is accompanied by an increased aversion to learning or the total neglect of music

opsimath: *n.*   one who learns late in life, like Secretaries of State who typically start learning after leaving office

optimist: *n.*   a person opening a DfES publication with hope of pleasure or profit

options: *n.pl.* sections of courses from which students may choose, on the cafeteria principle, an apt metaphor since the choice is spurious and the fare uniformly tasteless and unnourishing

ordinary: *adj.* patronizing characterization of most people by those who cannot conceive that it might more justly be applied to themselves

organization theory: *n.* amorphous study of the structure and functions of organizations, resting variously on reported practice, research, anecdote, technical assumptions and moral or aesthetic preference, of little use to someone in charge of a school or college

osmosis: *n.* gradual and unconscious assimilation of ideas, infomation and values, by analogy with the movement of a solution through a semi-permeable membrane: the unacknowledged recourse of education, given the failure of other methods, such as instruction

otherwise: *adv.* the way in which parents may see that their children are suitably educated if they think this unlikely in school

out: *v.* to state publicly, truthfully and gratuitously that someone is homosexual, confirming that malicious intolerance is not a monopoly of one kind of sexuality

overwork: *n.* pathological reaction to unsatisfactory circumstances

Oxbridge: *n.* composite term for the universities of Oxford and Cambridge (the alternative, Camford, never caught on), with high status among those now or formerly connected with them: they are still attractive to the young of a relatively narrow social and educational group, but are largely rejected by most eighteen-year-olds and mature people seeking higher education

Oxford: *pr.n.*   the best known provincial university in England

package: *n.*   set of proposals with hidden content, presented with an acceptable exterior: where possible it is wise to accept the wrapping and reject the rest

paedophile: *n.*   modern hobgoblin or foul fiend

paired reading: *n.*   method whereby two children who cannot read inhibit each other's learning to do so

PANDA: *n.*   unproductive creature consuming vast quantities of unnourishing feed, said to be an acronym for performance and assessment data for schools

paradox: *n.*   a saying which is offensive to all right-thinking persons, and true

parameter: *n.*   technical term in mathematics and statistics, wrongly used to mean a limit, as if confused with perimeter

parcel: *n.*   means favoured by the DfES for communicating with schools

parent: *n.*   (i) natural source of educational problems, occasionally contributing to a solution
   (ii) one who, having produced a child, expects a school to assume responsibility for it

parents' evening: *n.*   teachers' evening, a formal occasion on which teachers seek to place on pupils and parents the responsibility for the pupils' failure at school and make clear that both are expected to do better in future

parrot-fashion: *adj.*   characteristic of repetition which gains high marks because few methods of assessment can deal with anything more subtle

participation: *ger.*   taking part, being involved: usually confused by those in charge with compliance

pass: *v.*   gain enough marks in an examination to be awarded a qualification, emphasizing that the examination is a rite of passage rather than an aid to learning or an indication of its achievement

passmark: *n.*   arbitrarily chosen score in an examination occasioning temporary elation or discontent

pathetic fallacy: *n.*   sentimental attribution of human consciousness to inanimate nature, or in more modern times to computers and robots

payment by results: *n.*   nineteenth-century version of performance-related pay, which undermined the quality of teaching for a generation: the present version will be less damaging only because modern Ministers lack the stamina to persist with anything for more than five minutes

pedagogue: *n.*   in ancient Greece a slave who looked after his master's son; in modern England a slave who looks after innumerable sons, and daughters

pedagogy: *n.*   principles and practice of the inhibition of learning

pedant: *n.*   a person who thinks it matters that the Secretary of State is ignorant

peer group: *n.*   group of children of the same age, more influential on the outlook and behaviour of its members than parents, schools or mass media: successful schools understand the importance of establishing those conventions which trick them into compliance

penitence: *n.*   state of grace available to politicians but rarely entered by them

percentage: *n.*   proportion per hundred parts: its use is thought to imply precision, but this is usually spurious, as in a 'percentage of the school population' which adds nothing to 'some'

perception: *n.*   (i) becoming aware through the senses, once thought to be a pure and sure source of knowledge but accounts of this merely muddled empiricists, suggesting that perception is most useful as a check on one's hunches

(ii) comprehension, insight or intuition, best checked as in (i) above

(iii) all-purpose bludgeon for a convincing argument, as in 'that is just your perception'

performance-related pay: *n.*   (i) an award of £2000 paid to those teachers who can fill in a form, so called because the form-filling is such a performance

(ii) the use of instruments of appraisal to affect levels of salary: once this is done, everyone concentrates on the instruments rather than the persons, so that no truth about persons emerges and any possibility of improvement is scotched

period: *n.* division of the secondary school day in which a particular subject is taught: the end of a period, being arbitrary, is destructive of any interest or concentration that the subject may have inspired, and the practice of moving each form from room to room between periods produces only chaos

perseverance: *n.* obstinacy in what is thought to be a good cause

pessimist: *n.* one who believes or expects the worst, an entirely rational position but a debilitating one

pet: *n.* scourge of family life for the avoidance of which primary schools invented the nature table

phase: *n.* (i) a thing children go through, personally: 'it is only a phase' people say, as one torches the furniture
(ii) a thing children go through, institutionally, as in primary, secondary and further education: each of these phases serves a different end, respectively the basics, subjects and skills, rather than the pupils and students

phenomenology: *n.* a system of description and classification with different applications, depending on whether you listen to Kant, Hegel or Husserl

phenomenon: *n.* something perceptible, experienced and changeable, contrasted with an ideal or essence which is fixed but inaccessible: you can tell a lot about someone if you know which he prefers

philosophy: *n.* grand Greek word for thinking, often preceded by an adjective showing what is being thought about: thus, political philosophy is thinking about politics, educational philosophy is thinking about education, moral philosophy is thinking about morals, and philosophy unqualified is thinking about what nobody else is thinking about

phonics: *n.pl.*   a wheeze for inducing children to read by making them bark the sounds of separate letters or syllables, especially apt for a language with common words like bough, cough, dough, enough, ought, thorough and through

physical education: *n.*   training in sports and gymnastics having no lasting effect except a tendency to fat in later life

physics: *n.*   the science of matter and energy: despite its inclusion of such enticements as atomic, nuclear, particle and solid state studies, based on quantum theory, most secondary school students think it does not matter and can find no energy for its pursuit

pillory: *n.*   a rigid framework securing the heads and hands of offenders so that they might be ridiculed and abused, the model for measures said to improve the work and morale of teachers

plagiarism: *n.*   taking and using the words and ideas of another without letting on, much reviled and penalized in higher education: if done on a sufficient scale and with acknowledgement it is called scholarship

planets: *n.pl.*   bodies circling the sun, of which earth is inhabited by humankind, the rest by education Ministers

planning: *ger.*   the attempt to stop your successors from taking those decisions that they will be better placed to take than you are

play: *v.*   (i) divert or amuse oneself, an activity through which children learn and which is thus confined in schools to a quarter of an hour each morning and afternoon in conditions which make it impossible

(ii) contend against, an activity approved of and organized in formal education at all levels as an outlet for otherwise destructive aggression

playground: *n.*   bleak asphalt tract unconducive to repose or recreation

playtime: *n.*   supervised bullying

pleonasm: *n.*   too many words holding too little sense

pluralism: *n.*   arrangements for, or belief in, the distribution of power, both characteristics of educational administration until 1980: it is safe to predict that it will come into its own again, in some form, in the middle of this decade

poetry: *n.*   ambitious verse

political correctness: *n.*   politic conformity, a foible of feminism, multiculturalism and gay rights: for those who relish the evils that these movements excoriate it is politically correct to be politically incorrect

politician: *n.*   a person who seeks what he calls power by offering people what they want, believing that he knows what this is

politics: *n.*   the art of the plausible

polysyllable: *n.* ready recourse of flaccid thinkers and those who do not know what they are doing (see learning environment, diagnostic assessment, educational experience)

polytechnic: *n.* institution designated in the late 1960s explicitly to offer higher education in the service tradition: in the 1990s the polytechnics were allowed to call themselves universities to disguise the fact that the universities had become polytechnics

poor: *adj.* term of abuse employed as a substitute for help or spur to improvement, even less use when preceded by 'very'

populist: *n.* a person flattering the ignorant, thoughtless and apathetic, which in regard to any particular subject is most of us most of the time, by advancing ideas that were popular a generation ago

portrait: *n.* only noticeable result directly attributable to the tenure of most institutional heads

postgraduate: *adj.* (i) of studies undertaken after graduating which may be more taxing or interesting than those encountered before
(ii) of students kept by academic inertia in continuing study, being a rich source of papers by their supervisors

postmodern literature: *n.* books, essays and articles found on university booklists but not on the shelves of readers or of any but the most arcane libraries

postmodernism: *n.* a department store of reactions to modernism, and indeed tradition, in the arts and philosophy, never knowingly understood

postmodernist: *n.* one whose assertion that we can be confident of nothing is made with complete and unshakeable confidence

postnominals: *n.pl.* letters after one's name, the only certain consequence of a successful course of higher education and often the only desired outcome

power: *n.* the ability to do harm

powers and duties: *n.pl.* responsibilities of public bodies legally defined, distinguishing what may be done from what must: the tendency of modern Governments has been to burden other bodies with duties while removing their powers and to minimize their own duties while inflating their powers

practice: *n.* the fourth category of communication from the DfES offering off-the-peg solutions to problems created by DfES decisions (see circular)

pre-school playgroup: *n.* regular supervised play of a group of children arranged by their parents who valued their own involvement: between the obsessive demands of health and safety on the one hand and the intrusion of educational professionals, bureaucrats and politicians on the other, the practice has been effectively abolished

preach: *v.* give unwanted moral instruction or exhortation: once the prerogative of the clergy, it is now rife among politicians, officials, journalists, inspectors, pop stars and headteachers

prefect: *n.* a pupil given limited power over others, now a shrunken figure devoted to stopping sprinting in the corridors and thus a weak barrier against chaos in many schools

prejudice: *n.* the irrefutable basis of Government policy

preparatory school: *n.* one which charges fees for promising to get its pupils into public schools, a promise that can hardly fail to be met since there are always some public schools with empty places

pressure: *n.* urgent claim or demand, moral force or burdensome condition, invented by those in charge to inhibit independence and responsibility

prestige project: *n.* building put up by a vice-chancellor on the make, its funding coming partly from Government, partly from donors and mostly from the forgone salaries of staff and the fees of students denied what they thought they were paying for

prestigious: *adj.* someone or something of which few have heard

primary school: *n.* school in which teachers, fired by a respect for pupils, are required to secure their resemblance to circus animals doing ingenious but demeaning tricks for the satisfaction of the populace

private school: *n.* school founded and run for the pleasure and profit of the proprietor

privilege: *n.* (i) anything that you have that I want
(ii) what minorities actually want when they demand equality

prize: *n.* bribe to secure desired behaviour, highly economical since it is given, not to all who are to be influenced, but to one or two only

prize-giving: *n.*   ceremony at which teachers recognize those students who comply and conform: for many this will be the last recognition they will attract in their lives

problem: *n.*   (i) routine exercise in mathematics, repeated practice in which it is romantically expected to produce understanding

(ii) in learning, that which arises when one discovers one's ignorance and determines to remedy it, when the problem is how to get from one state of affairs to another: people often speak of the problem of illiteracy, but illiteracy is just a state and becomes a problem only when someone proposes to do something about it

problem child: *n.*   difficult issue

productivity: *n.*   demand by those in charge that others do better as their circumstances are worsened

professional: *adj.*   implying a relationship with a client in which the interests of the client are paramount: this is difficult in formal education since the client ought to be the child, but parents and employers also have claims, and because a teacher is seldom dealing with just one child at a time; but this is no excuse for the widespread neglect of the principle to the detriment of both children and their teachers

professional development: *n.*   a phrase to which it is hard to attach meaning: development implies improvement, but this can seldom be seen to arise from the activities said to promote it

professor: *n.*   one who professes as distinct from one who does

profile: *n.*   one-dimensional view of a person, used and advocated by educators who fear complex human nature

programmed learning: *n.*   mechanically based system relying on stimulus-response (q.v.) which was once advocated as an aid to human learning, but nothing has been heard of it lately

progress: *n.*   (i) any change, however deleterious, that has contributed to the present state of affairs
(ii) any change, however silly or shortlived, introduced by a Government
(iii) the name those in charge give to the chaos they occasion

progressive: *adj.*   characteristic of a school movement, begun in 1889, feared and loathed for its assumption that education should start from where pupils and students are so that they might benefit from it, discrediting itself periodically by romantic child-centredness and anti-intellectualism

projection: *n.*   extension of the line of a graph beyond the point where anything is known in order to dismay or gull the public

propaganda: *n.*   education after school

prospects: *n.pl.*   those things which education is said to improve, the truth of which is in inverse relation to the numbers of the educated

prospectus: *n.*   from the Latin combining the ideas of a distant view and a look forward, hence a brochure offering a view of a course, school or college some distance from reality, often concentrating on tradition

psychologist: *n.*   one who studies the mind, which neurologists typically say does not exist

psychology: *n.*   (i) a vast portmanteau subject covering disparate activities, including brain science, intelligence and aptitude testing, behavioural studies and theories of personal, social and industrial interaction, all of these having a philosophical or a curative bias, and most of their practitioners being at odds with one another: so far psychology has proved oddly inconsequential for education

(ii) character or disposition, as in the psychology of the individual, recommended by Jeeves as a study for those wishing to be socially manipulative

public opinion: *n.*   (i) settled habit of mind in a given population, often right and reliable

(ii) answers to tendentious questions from pollsters and politicians, usually wrong and irresponsible

public school: *n.*   school which excludes the children of the public, devoting itself instead to increasing the advantages of those of the rich and powerful, an inevitably and legally charitable activity

public–private partnership: *n.*   (i) administrative and financial relationship reminiscent of that between the body and the leech or the tourist and the pickpocket

(ii) wheeze for conferring the benefits of free enterprise on the public services, so that they can match the *Herald of Free Enterprise* at Zeebrugge, the northbound train at Hatfield or the sale of duff pension schemes

publish: *v.*   prologue to perdition: 'publish and be damned' (1st Duke of Wellington), but teachers in

English universities are damned if they do not, and teachers in schools are expected to have better things to do

punctuation: *n.*   the dots, dashes, points and squiggles representing stops or pauses in writing, essential for sense, clarity and elegance, but once so overdone by pedants as now to be scorned and neglected

pupa: *n.*   grub or maggot, torpidly waiting to be an insect (cf. pupil)

pupil: *n.*   a dependent person who is taught, quite different from one who learns, for which independence is required

pure: *adj.*   unsullied by usefulness

QAAHE: *n.*   unpronounceable acronym for Quality Assessment Agency for Higher Education, a body which monitors the contents of filing cabinets in universities and colleges

QCA: *n.*   unsatisfactory acronym, pronounced 'quacker', of the Qualifications and Curriculum Agency: its name reveals that it regards education as a preparation not for life but for tests, and it pursues this fatuity with energy

quadrangle: *n.*   rectangular courtyard with buildings on all four sides, the scarcity of which in a university greatly undermines its reputation

qualification: *n.*   (i) attribute required to do a job or assume a status

(ii) scrap of paper or parchment purporting to represent (i): qualifications are what educational institutions provide in lieu of learning

qualify: *v.*   (i) restrict, enfeeble or moderate

(ii) take a course tending to (i) above in order to be accepted into a profession

quality: *n.*   (i) officially approved but vague characteristic involving neither achievement nor value: in higher education it is identified mostly by quantity

(ii) when used barbarously as an adjective, as in quality time, it can mean good, effective, valuable, rich or, most often, nothing

quality assurance: *n.*   an impossibility, since the only thing of which one can be assured is failure

quality control: *n.*   system for securing that, if there has to be quality, there should not be too much of it

question: *n.*   (i) interrogative remark to elicit information: when permitted to students it may assist learning

(ii) interrogative remark or other instruction used by teachers and examiners to see how far students remember what they have been told: of little assistance to the learning of either teachers or students

quiz: *n.*   a game whose popularity derives from its resemblance to education as most people remember it; played in public houses and television studios, it reveals how much the participants know and how little use this is

quorum: *n.* the number of members of a committee needed to let the chairman have his own way without personal risk

racism: *n.* a principle on which inadequate people hate their betters

radical: *adj.* attribute of any proposal or course of action which changes enough to preclude judgement as to whether it is better or worse than what it replaces

rate of return: *n.* economic notion once fashionably if naïvely applied to education with inconclusive results

rational: *adj.* (i) of persons, thoughtful
(ii) of actions, sensible and well thought out, to be avoided by practical persons on the ground that people are not (i) above

rationale: *n.* later explanation and excuse for a course of action taken without thought

rationalist: *n.* one who thinks that knowledge of what exists can be gained from thinking about it, where an empiricist thinks it comes to one

reactionary: *n.* one whose ideas are so out of date that their time has come again

read: *v.* (i) make out written or printed words
(ii) make sense of something written or printed, for profit or pleasure: this is seldom the consequence of

officially prescribed lessons in primary schools, because of their authors' obsession with (i) above

reader: *n.*   (i) a book for learning to read with, distinguishable from one that a pupil might want to read
  (ii) pupil who can read and is prepared to do so in the books which a school provides

readership: *n.*   academic post below professorship, thus requiring its holder to continue writing

reading: *ger.*   (i) second of the 'basics' or three Rs: the Government's favoured method of teaching it largely eschews meaning
  (ii) ideally a spur to thought, more often a substitute for it

reason: *n.*   (i) faculty of thought
  (ii) excuse for irrational behaviour

recognition: *n.*   that which formal assessment accords to trivial performance and withholds from significant achievement

reductionism: *n.*   attempt to understand or manage complexity by making it simple

re-education: *n.*   the attempt to substitute the evils of one kind of education for those of another

referee: *n.*   (i) person asked by the editor of a learned journal to say whether a submitted article threatens the current orthodoxy and should thus be rejected: this can be done either by agreeing that the article is interesting, well-argued and well written but adding that it ignores irrelevant, ill-written and tedious works by the referee and others, or by arguing that a different article altogether would be preferable and that in any case two books, one of them by the referee, are absent from the references

(ii) person writing to an appointing body in terms which may be held to justify the bad appointment they have made

(iii) one whose decisions in a game provoke children to behave as badly as adults

refereed journal: *n.*   publication designed to enable academics to meet the vacuous demands of the research assessment exercise while securing, through referees, the exclusion of matter uncongenial to the prejudices of the editor and advisory board

references: *n.pl.*   list of books and articles, appended to a learned article, which the author has not read and has no intention of reading but which excuses the vacuity of the preceding text

reform: *n.*   (i) meddle and muddle
(ii) what a Government does to any popular and useful institution so as to limit its scope and effectiveness

register: *n.*   unreliable guide to attendance at a school

relativism: *n.*   the view that there can be no reason to prefer one theory, argument, morality or culture to another, captured in the mindless retort, 'That's just your opinion': relativism happily defeats itself, since if it is true there can be no reason to accept it

religious education: *n.*   presentation to children of beliefs held in abhorrence by most of the human race

report: *n.*   formal statement to parents made by a school about the effect on a child of what the school has offered, carrying the message that any shortcomings must be the fault of the child, if not the parents

research: *n.*   substitute for remedial action

resources: *n.pl.*   money

responsibility: *n.*   attribute of a teaching post attracting a derisory salary increment

results: *n.pl.*   that which the children of England are required to produce at school in order to secure the political career of a Secretary of State, than which no purpose can be more important and ennobling

retirement party: *n.*   ceremony at which staff staying at a school offer wine, crisps and good wishes to those leaving: in lucky schools the former outnumber the latter

reverence: *n.*   the proper attitude of teachers confronted by an official utterance

revision: *n.*   memorizing quickly what has not been mastered after intensive teaching

rights: *n.pl.*   (i) the sure possession of the ignorant, as in 'I know my rights'
    (ii) claims that are recognized by enough other people: the demand for such recognition is insatiable, and granting it in a particular case may be right or wrong

rising fives: *n.pl.*   four-year-olds: the expression reveals the educational habit of regarding children, not as they are, but only as incomplete versions of their older selves

ritual: *n.*   ceremony in prescribed form, sometimes believed by its participants to affect themselves or the world: common in education (see, for example, SATS, GCSE)

role: *n.*   that which people are said to have if they have neither purpose nor function

rostrum: *n.*   platform for public speaking: the one in the Roman forum was decorated with the prows of captured ships and was thus known as the rostra (plural), but this seems to have been turned into the singular by a helpful and misinformed pedant

rote: *n.*   'mere habituation ... repetition, unintelligent memory' (COD), a method of learning held in awe by those who have learned nothing recently, if ever: people often recommend that children are made to get poetry by rote, not realizing that this is different from getting it by heart

rules: *n.pl.*   directions provided for the guidance of the wise and the worship of the foolish

sabbatical: *n.*   year, term or other period of leave from formal academic duties, after the Levitical injunction to leave fields uncultivated every seventh year

satchel: *n.*   old-fashioned receptacle for what has been taught: most of this goes directly from the blackboard or whiteboard into a bag without touching the pupil

SATs: *n.pl.*   (i) standard assessment tasks: a means of central control introduced by the Education Act 1988 to inhibit teachers from thinking for themselves and children from surpassing mediocrity

(ii) in the USA, scholastic aptitude tests, devices by which universities reject applicants, much criticized since some of those rejected are otherwise privileged

scholar: *n.*   a learned person, one who enjoys the approval of those whose opinions he respects

scholarly: *adj.*   having a conscientious tendency to flatter, by repeated reference, those who are to judge one's thesis or other work

scholarship: *n.*   (i) a device which, if gained, enables one to go to school or college without paying

(ii) an activity which enables one to be paid for being in a college or university, but there are other activities which work just as well and are less onerous

scholastic: *adj.*   egregiously hyperacademic

school: *n.*   (i) custodial institution without the comfort of individual cells but with a planned programme of routine and unproductive work for the inmates tempered by exercise, entertainment and religious observance

(ii) establishment largely blamed by parents, moralists and politicians for not arresting social change or avoiding its conseqences

(iii) institution variously thought of as a seminary for a sect, a vehicle for job training, a remedy for social ills or saviour of the planet, but which can be useful only as a safe place to learn

(iv) one of the main generators of traffic congestion

(v) institution to which children are sent to be fattened up: they remain inedible, however

(vi) a shoal or large group of fish moving as one, thus easily netted: an apt metaphor for some of the other meanings

school board: *n.*   elected body of ratepayers which built, staffed and maintained elementary schools in England between 1870 and 1902: as soon as their success became conspicuous they were abolished

school dinner: *n.*   ceremony once productive of civilized manners and unprecedented health in school children, now much etiolated and leading to obesity

school phobia: *n.*   a misnomer, since a phobia is an irrational fear, and school can be injurious to mental and physical health

school refuser: *n.*   child who dislikes school and resolves to have none of it, but instead of taking to truancy makes a stand and thus gives trouble to the authorities

school rules: *n.pl.*   injunctions and prohibitions, often seemingly trivial or irrational, but serving the vital and rational end of social order: where control is not exercised by such means, order can be maintained only by penalties, which are ineffective

school secretary: *n.*   person in sole charge of a school, dealing with all the serious problems of pupils and students, teachers, parents and other visitors, the dinner ladies and above all the head teacher

schoolboys/girls: *n.pl.*   the chief educators of children at school

schooling: *n.*   dressage for children

schoolmaster: *n.*   apparent leader of a group of fish, hence a male teacher

schoolmistress: *n.*   a female teacher: this term and the related schoolmaster are asserted by the politically correct to be offensive, so see schoolteacher

schoolteacher: *n.*   one who teaches in a school: the use of this word, in place of the simpler term teacher, avoids the implication that those in schools are in the same profession as those in higher education, which would never do

science: *n.*   (i) one of the most glorious achievements of the human mind and spirit
(ii) once thought of as the pedestrian accumulation of certainties, now as a congeries of unrefuted conjectures, not based on but tested by observation and experiment
(iii) a mindless succession of routine procedures required of students in secondary school laboratories

sciolism: *n.*   any discussion of education, or indeed anything else, in public houses, dinner parties and Parliament

scroll: *n.*   roll of parchment, an inadequate forerunner of the book: used as a verb it means to move a text about a computer screen, emphasizing the huge step back from the book this technology has taken

scrutiny: *n.*   close study: its major perversions are inspection, examination and appraisal

secondary education: *n.*   that which is indispensible for pure foolishness (F. Nietzsche)

secondary modern school: *n.*   institution romantically designed to offer secondary education to all without the aridity of the grammar school curriculum but no match, in the end, for academic and social pretension

secondary school: *n.*   school in which teachers, fired by a respect for students, are required to turn them into economic units or instruments of state

Secretary of State: *n.*   a member of the government, endowed *ex officio* with every god-like feature except the power to do good: it is not that Secretaries of State think or intend evil; they just do it

selection: *n.*   system of entry to schools which removes choice from parents and gives it to the schools

self: *n.*   one's own identity: when used by teachers in a combining form, as in self-confidence, self-image, self-worth and self-assurance, it signals sentimentality about students rather than rigour about their learning

self-discipline: *n.*   (i) that capacity which enables students to do what somebody else wants without being told
   (ii) self-command: in formal education there are so many other commands that this one is rarely exercised

self-expression: *n.*   education through graffiti, the grim object of child-centred education: unless one expresses a great deal more than oneself, one cannot learn much

semester: *n.*   one of the divisions of an academic year that is divided into two, introduced into English universities without abolishing the alternative division into three terms, thus demonstrating the faddiness, timidity and muddle of academic life

seminar: *n.* once a small group of students meeting, with the guidance of a tutor, to discuss texts, theories, work in progress and so on, now either a tutorial in a poverty-stricken university or a lecture in an overcrowded room

senior management team: *n.* group of between two and six people in a school who decide to do what the Secretary of State requires

serious weaknesses: *n.pl.* orotund inspectorial phrase for unsubstantiated disapproval

sex: *n.* that which distinguishes men from women, of much less importance than conventional people think

sex education: *n.* according to conservative commentators, the whole curriculum of schools today, hence the attempt to exclude that part of it relating to homosexuality so as to make room for maths, history and so on

sexism: *n.* discrimination on the basis of sex, except the oppression of men by women

shame culture: *n.* social control relying on external sanctions, contrasted with guilt culture, relying on an internal conviction of sin: the terms are no longer current in anthropology where they began, but the concepts are alive in those educational administrators who cannot imagine other reasons why professional people should want to do well

show trial: *n.* procedure using judicial forms and rigged criteria designed to humiliate and then destroy its victims, the model of which school inspections are now based

significant: *adj.*   having meaning or importance: when qualified by 'statistically', having no meaning or importance

simile: *n.*   a comparison in one respect of like with unlike, for effect, as in bureaucracy flourishing like the green bay tree

sink school: *n.*   originally a school into which children trickled from a wide area because it had places and others were full: given that such children were commonly those excluded elsewhere, without English, refugees or from unstable homes, the school was not only heroic in itself but the condition for 'success' in other schools, but now, because of journalistic carelessness, the term has become an unjust synonym for an unsuccessful school

sins: *n.pl.*   moral offences, seven of which are deadly, viz. pride, envy, anger, covetousness, sloth, gluttony and lust, the first four being actively promoted by the Government's tests and league tables, as is even the fifth, in the form of accidie or spiritual and intellectual sloth: there must surely be a working party of civil servants even now considering how to develop the last two

Sisyphean: *adj.*   chief characteristic of the task imposed on teachers by the key stages of the National Curriculum

sixth form: *n.*   class of students in a school following year eleven, obviously, offering two years' preparation for A level: it is traditionally a time when students have the chance of serious intellectual relationships with a fair number of intelligent people who have their interests at heart, an experience few of them find repeated at university

sixth form college: *n.*   school with a sixth form but without the rest of the school

skill: *n.*   (i) enviable facility in making or doing
   (ii) set of operations, limited in scope, importance, current application and reward, compulsorily acquired by those desiring a state benefit

slow learners: *n.pl.*   officials with a pat solution

small school: *n.*   an object of desire in parents and hatred in officials

society: *n.*   a nonentity: when M. Thatcher famously said that there was no such thing as society, she showed only her inability to distinguish a thing from a concept

sophisticate: *v.*   render (a person) less innocent, for example by rape or education

sophisticated: *adj.*   ignorantly or trivially knowing

sows' ears: *n.pl.*   traditionally unpromising material for the manufacture of silk purses, metaphorically an excuse for educational failure: many institutions which get fine silk still do not produce purses

special: *adj.*   unwelcome, as in special needs, special measures

special measures: *n.pl.*   inspectors' demand that a school pull its socks up, so as to be in a convenient position for further thrashing

special needs: *n.pl.* mealy-mouthed phrase disguising a shift of blame for educational failure from schools and public authorities to children: 'If a system or method fails with a significant number of children, it is the system or method that must change' (K. Hickey), but provision for special needs is directed to changing the children, leaving the institutional failure intact and implying that most children who are not special are negligible

specialist: *n.* person who knows nothing about most things and not enough about one, of little use as a teacher

specialist school: *n.* the latest fraudulent title in the pretence that education is generally improving because some schools, generously funded and selecting some of their pupils, can be said to do better than others

specialize: *v.* to limit or constrain one's interests, so as to limit and constrain one's study

speech: *n.* that which in most people precedes thought by anything from half a second to a lifetime

spelling: *ger.* tedious and largely pointless branch of the school subject of writing, insisted on by pedants because it can be awarded ticks and crosses which when counted up produce a mark

spin: *n.* politicians' tribute to the power of truth

spine: *n.* the main structural support of a skeleton: a pay spine will support only a skeletal teacher

sponsor: *n.*   person or corporation with more money than sense, induced by a Government to relieve it of the duty to provide a school

sport: *n.*   (i) over-energetic and ineffective substitute for healthy living
  (ii) acrimony partly contained by rules
  (iii) the point of organization at which games, already no fun, become harmful: people say that sport is character-building, but the character it builds is that of the egomaniac

staff room: *n.*   depressing sitting room in a school, housing a photocopier and coffee machine, a place of respite rather than relaxation (cf. common room)

stamina: *n.*   staying power, an academic virtue: the word is of course plural, of stamen, and derives from the threads of life spun out by the Fates, which is very encouraging to remember

standard: *n.*   an exemplary level of performance, determined by the means used to measure it: it offers no information about the capacity beyond the standard of those who reach it nor of the other capacities of those who do not, and is thus otiose for educational purposes

standards: *n.pl.*   steps towards an increase in the gross national mind

statement: *n.*   list of promises made by a local education authority to children who resist instuction more than most, usually offering yet more instruction: the promises are pitched low for ease of keeping, but this is the only occasion in the formal system where the wishes of parents and pupils have to be sought and considered

statistics: *n.pl.*   (i) the replacement of reason by arithmetic

(ii) the third level of lying (trad.)

(iii) analysis by numbers, more reliable but less informative than anecdote

(iv) tables of figures relating to a subject or organization: those put out by Government are presented on the bikini principle, in that they display what is thought to be tempting and conceal what is essential

status: *n.*   social evaluation distinguishable from wealth, power and worth, craved by those who have none of these

statutory instrument: *n.*   secondary legislation: the additional opportunity provided for in primary legislation for detailed meddling control by the Secretary of State

stereotype: *n.*   metal printing plate once made from a papier-mâché mould, hence a standardized image of a social group, as when one says of politicians, 'They are all the same'

stimulus-response: *n.*   a common enough occurrence in the relationship between an animal and its environment, but inadequate in itself to produce even animal learning: this lower-order activity was once thought to offer a basis for human learning, especially when provoked by machines, but it is now seen to have been a waste of time

stoic: *n.*   one who appears or professes himself to be indifferent equally to pleasure and pain: in education it is the latter that offers stoics the more scope

streaming: *ger.*   practice of placing children in groups, or streams, according to some measure of ability, based on the commonsense notion that they will all thereby learn better, for which there is no convincing evidence

strike: *n.*   a programme for advancing one's own interests by directly injuring them: the only recourse of a union

student: *n.*   one who is expected to learn by listening and reading, showing what he has learned by writing something (cf. apprentice)

student body: *n.*   all the students in an institution, usually a thoughtless mob, since only an individual student can have a head

student evaluation: *n.*   system of staff appraisal based on the theory that those who scarcely know how to learn will best judge how to teach

study: *n.*   that of which much, according to the Preacher, is a weariness of the flesh (Ecclesiastes 12.12)

study skills: *n.pl.*   tricks and dodges taught to students to enable them to cram more effectively

subject: *n.*   (i) branch of knowledge arbitrarily delineated to protect the interests of its practitioners: in education the problems of the subject are held to be of more importance and interest than the problems of the pupils or students

(ii) stock-in-trade of the secondary school or university teacher, but not enough to do the job properly

subject association: *n.* organization of teachers to lobby for their subject at the expense of those of others

subject coordinator: *n.* otiose post created in primary schools so as to intrude an inapt career stucture, based on the false assumption that learning derives from subjects rather than problems

success: *n.* a favourable outcome, usually of an examination, which is fully relished only if it is denied to others

suicide: *n.* extreme ingratitude from one who has benefited from inspection

summative assessment: *n.* (i) tiresome circumlocution for examination
(ii) a congeries of formative assessments

Sunday school: *n.* classes for children arranged by a church or chapel at an hour on Sundays otherwise unfilled by services, so as to keep some of its adult members out of mischief

superhead: *n.* headteacher from a successful school transferred on a higher salary to an unsuccessful one and retiring within a year from nervous prostration: a silly name for a silly idea

supervisor: *n.* an academic supposedly overseeing the work of a graduate student, but usually overlooking it

suppression: *n.* the instinctive reponse of authority to something it dislikes or does not understand

surprise: *n.*   a word once liable to catachresis, but usage has overcome this, thus destroying the story of the professor of English found in bed with a student by his wife who exclaimed, 'Well, I am surprised,' to which her husband replied, 'No, dear, I am surprised; you are astonished'

swot: *n.*   child who works hard at school and is smug about it (obs.): these days those who work at all take pains to conceal the fact

syllabus: *n.*   a mistake, since the word should be sittybus, miscopied by a careless monk in the middle ages, but this is not the only centuries-old mistake to be a foundation of formal education: a sittybus was a parchment strip giving a title and author, so a syllabus is a list of subjects or components of a subject, in contrast to a curriculum which derives from and has the characteristics of a horse race (Maths is English schools' Beecher's Brook)

synergy: *n.*   assumed potential of two separate bodies to work better after a merger, seldom realized and never after amalgamating schools or colleges, recovery from which takes at least five years

synonym: *n.*   antonym of antonym

tactics: *n.pl.*   clever manoeuvres that undo a strategy, as the literacy hour undermines the design to make children more literate

task force: *n.*   a committee dealing with a subject with which some politician means to imply his urgent concern

taste: *n.*   the ability to make discerning judgements about intellectual or aesthetic matters, now held to be élitist and thus banished from the National Curriculum

taught: *past part.*   served right

tautology: *n.*   words added, or the act of adding words, without adding meaning, as when the Government claims to have 'achieved results', since a result is simply something that has been achieved: the phrase reminds this lexicographer of a lot in a Swindon auction sale described as 'box of contents'

teach: *v.*   (i) encumber with help
   (ii) indoctrinate or oppress: to teach someone a lesson is to do something nasty to him
   (iii) instruct another: G. B. Shaw's most misquoted remark, 'He who can, does. He who cannot, teaches', is a great comfort to all those people who can do neither

teachable: *adj.*   coming from a good home

teacher: *n.*   (i) one whose occupation is teaching but whose hopes are for learning
   (ii) one who can give to students a sense of confidence, the blessing of criticism and the keys to knowledge and capability: some teachers despair, believing that they cannot organize families or society and cannot compete with the mass media, but nothing can beat a competent teacher when serious learning is required

teaching: *n.*   (i) a set of procedures, perfected since the beginning of time, designed to prevent learning

(ii) continuous and ill-founded educational experiment

teaching method: *n.*   any one of numerous sets of procedures adopted by teachers in the hope of inducing learning, of which some do not work at all and none work with all children or in the hands of all teachers: skill in teaching resides in tirelessly trying them all to see which serves whom best

technical college: *n.*   (obs.) institution in which most people who had any education after school received it, largely unknown to policy makers and when thought of, despised: technical colleges were the founding institutions of most universities, a fact which the universities prefer to forget

term: *n.*   division of the academic year, separated from others by vacations and called Spring, Summer or Autumn, never Winter: it has been found convenient for millennia to have three terms a year, but a proposal to have four, five or six can periodically be expected from bankrupt policy makers

terror: *n.*   emotion experienced by officials and inspectors confronted by independence of mind

tertiary college: *n.*   sixth form college with some extra and useful courses

test: *n.*   pot used for assaying metals, hence metaphorically a means of determining the existence, nature, quality, correctness or genuineness of something: in education, though not in metallurgy, only the faults, flaws and impurities are thought to be of interest

textbook: *n.*   sole source for essays and examination answers: the anti-educational consequences of this might be mitigated if students were asked to read and use it critically, but alas they seldom are

thesis: *n.*   some 70,000 words on a topic worth 700, impossible to turn into a publishable, still less a readable, book

think: *v.*   (i) exercise the mind to some purpose, that which is education's oft-claimed purpose to promote and its universal practice to prevent
   (ii) have in mind: people mistakenly distinguish between what we think and what we know, believing the latter to be more certain, but what we know is only what we think that seems not to be false

thinker: *n.*   a suspicious and dangerous character who requires constant distraction by a good teacher

thinking: *ger.*   mental activity mainly performed with words or other symbols (J. Haldane) having a modest place in education compared with reading, listening, remembering and repeating

thought: *n.*   that which enables one to learn from one's mistakes before one has made them

thoughtfulness: *n.*   calm reflection, careful reasoning, consideration for others: not a whiff of any of this is required in the school curriculum

three Rs: *n.pl.*   appallingly arch hypocorisma for the 'basics' of reading, 'riting and 'rithmetic, the curriculum on which children are required to expend their spirit between the ages of five and seven

times: *conj.*   multiplied by, demonstrating that multiplication is repeated addition: four times five is four, five times

timetable: *n.*   the only, unchanging and unchallenged principle on which secondary education is based

toddler: *n.*   small child learning to walk, largely uninstructed, and succeeding because unaware that staggering and falling down constitute failure

totalitarian: *adj.*   regulating, as a Government, every aspect of life: English education is not yet fully benefiting from such a system, but important strides have been made in its direction, from the detailed control of the activities of seven-year-olds to the show trial element of inspections

trade school: *n.*   institution for training in a simple skill, so as to enable people to sell themselves: university graduates who have no skills sell themselves at a higher price

tradition: *n.*   last year's innovation

traditional: *adj.*   of a settled tendency in education to insist on well-known methods, 'the basics' and a common content to the curriculum which all children should learn, discrediting itself periodically by disputes about method and content and by the realization that many children are learning very little

train: *n.*   guide, control or exercise (someone) for a specific end, purpose or pattern, like a rose on a trellis

trainee: *n.*   one stultified by training

trainer: *n.* one who makes a living inducing animals to do demeaning tricks or otherwise perform to order, using the insights derived from rat psychology, or one who applies similar techniques to children, athletes, musicians and others

training: *ger.* drill or discipline based on the discredited assumptions of faculty psychology

training college: *n.* institution for instructing teachers for the children of the poor (obs.)

transmission: *n.* process by which teaching produces learning, though nobody can say how this is supposed to happen, and there is no evidence that it does

transparency: *n.* (i) quality required of the operations of those employed, so that they can be better controlled, but not of those in charge, lest they be held accountable
   (ii) acetate sheet used for projecting banalities onto a screen upside down

transport: *n.* combination of devices and systems offering the experience of travel and the illusion of progress, an effective means of prolonging the school day and a support to the illusion of parental choice

treatise: *n.* systematic written exposition, discussion or argument, largely replaced in academic life by the thesis, dissertation, journal articles or textbooks

trees: *n.pl.* the natural allies of bad architects: the crassest school building can seem acceptable if its surroundings be sufficiently bosky, so in architects' plans, perspectives and models representations of trees proliferate

tried and tested: *adj.* introduced long ago by chance or mistake, now thoughtlessly applied

truancy: *n.* practical criticism, sometimes ill-considered, of what school offers

truism: *n.* statement that is both tedious and true

trust: *n.* (i) reliance on or confidence in: like loyalty it is demanded most loudly by those who give it most sparingly
(ii) a quality of which the habitual lack is more damaging than the disappointment arising from its incautious exercise

truth: *n.* a vital aspiration: those who have it cannot be sure that they do, and those who are convinced that they have it almost certainly do not, and hence persecute others

TTA: *pr.n.* Teacher Training Agency: rightly assuming that the stultification of children requires the prior stultification of teachers, this organization depends upon its own fatuity to avoid serious damage to either

tuition: *n.* (i) that which is given by anyone teaching, readily and completely visible and assessable: those taught might in a sense be said to receive the tuition, were it not for the fact that what they actually receive is unknown and indeed unknowable, and assessments designed to discover this address only trivialities
(ii) in universities in the United States of America, tuition is what you pay, not what you pay for, still less get

tutee: *n.* the victim of tutoring, a similar construction to amputee, a vile neologism for an unwelcome state

tutor: *n.*   (i) one responsible for the learning of another (from late Latin, tueri, to watch over)

(ii) person to whose wisdom and diligence the success of students is due, unlike their failures which are their own responsibility and are thus punishable by the tutor

tutorial: *n.*   meeting between teacher and student in which neither listens to the other

undergraduate: *n.*   one enrolled on a course with the expectation of gaining a first degree, similar to a student except that the latter may also be studying

underlining: *ger.*   mutilation of books by the semi-studious: from the evidence they leave it is clear that those who underline never finish the book

understanding: *n.*   ability to apprehend and comprehend, intelligence, judgement: not required to be displayed in formal education until doctorate level and often not even then

uniform: *n.*   (i) the informal wear of the young

(ii) clothing designed to make school children look alike which succeeds only in emphasizing their differences

(iii) oddly effective form of social control (and see school rules)

uniformity: *n.*   the daily desire and nightly dream of an official

unintended: *adj.*   the only guaranteed kind of consequence of policy, legislation or institutions: when unintended consequences are benign they are claimed to have been originally purposed, when malign they are unacknowledged

university: *n.*   once, the whole universe; now the whole body of teachers and students thought to be pursuing the higher branches of learning in an insitution set up for this purpose, mistaking themselves for the former

university of life: *n.*   what unacademic people claim to have been educated in, a misnomer: polytechnic of life is more like it, but any academic life is a contradiction in terms

university press: *n.*   publisher of books which nobody would dream of reading

vacation: *n.*   period in the year when the formally organized work of an institution is suspended in order, according to academics, that the real work can be done

value judgement: *n.*   prejudice

values: *n.*   moral aspirations, invoked to conceal the absence of proposals, policies, ideas, action, thought or any other desirable response to a pressing problem

variety: *n.*   quality or condition acceptable in tinned foods, up to a limit of 57, but not in pupils and students

verbal: *adj.* of, or using, words; used by journalists when they mean oral

vertical grouping: *n.* organization of infant-school classes on grounds other than age: rational but hopeless in today's circumstances

very good: *adj.* vacuous and patronizing commendation by a generous assessor, inspector or teacher

vice-chancellor: *n.* person of the highest character and qualification whose virtues inhibit him from defending a university against the oppressions of Government

village college: *n.* educational institution based on the romantic principle that education is for everybody, not just for the young who are not permitted to avoid it

virtual: *adj.* as near as makes no difference, except when it makes all the difference, as in a virtual first class degree

virtual reality: *n.* (i) real simulation, especially by computer
  (ii) the nearest that politicians, officials and inspectors get to knowing what happens in education

virtue: *n.* moral excellence or righteousness which in oneself is insufficiently appreciated by others

virtues: *n.pl.* moral excellencies, of which three are theological – faith, hope and charity – four are cardinal – justice, prudence, temperance and fortitude: educational policy lacks all seven

viva: *n.*   conversation between a candidate and an examiner, being an attempt, sometimes vain, to give the former the benefit of the doubt

vocabulary: *n.*   all the words known, understood and used by a person, of interest to educators only when noticeably sparse

waste-paper basket: *n.*   inevitable and proper repository for advice, guidance and statements of best practice

well-read: *adj.*   having done much reading without forgetting too much of it

what works: *n.*   what a politician, imperfectly remembering his own schooldays, imagines ought to work

white paper: *n.*   once a statement of Government policy and the means, including legislation, for implementing it; now a large-format book, unreadable because of the dazzle from its glossy paper, the varying but always inapt width of its columns, the breaking up of its text into coloured boxes, the irrelevance of its pictures and its impenetrable prose, all designed to conceal the intellectual and practical bankruptcy of its authors

whole-class teaching: *n.*   unpromising proceeding, since while a whole class may be taught only individuals can learn

wisdom: *n.*   attribute claimed by people of high status who lack others, like cleverness, capability, good sense, knowledge and experience

woman: *n.*   traditionally a world ruler, since 'the hand that rocks the cradle...rules the world' (W. Wallace), but this claim is rejected by feminists: nevertheless women sometimes make good mothers, which men seldom do

words: *n.pl.*   elements of speech and writing for transferring an idea from one mind to another (G. Young), except when mishandled by their users, which is normal: formal education is little help here, since it values neither the ideas of the learners nor any practice in giving them expression

workshop: *n.*   something other than a shop in which no work is done

world class: *adj.*   of the quality of education which English Ministers want for a half of what it costs where they think it exists

writing: *ger.*   (i) letters on a surface so grouped as to convey meaning
    (ii) the second of the 'basics' or three Rs, meant to ensure than children can manipulate (i) above
    (iii) any literary composition, precluded in schools by the methods they are forced to use for (ii) above

wrong, the: *n.*   place from which people tend to produce their best arguments

year: *n.*   (i) grouping of schoolchildren according to age, an irrational proceeding to which much of the damage done by formal education can be attributed

(ii) twelve months beginning in the calendar in January, in finance in April and in academic life in September or October

year seven: *n.*   first year or form in a secondary school where the learning of the preceding six years is systematically undone

yes: *sent. sub.*   acknowledgement, affirmation, consent, agreement, approval: a word whose use is almost always fruitful and thus used sparingly in education.

youth: *n.*   condition of promise and paranoia for which there is no cure, but it goes away of its own accord

zero: *n.*   the nothing that, in mathematics at least, makes all possible, indeed in mathematics you cannot know anything unless you understand nothing

Afterword

Education is an activity that occasions both hope and despair, sometimes alternately and sometimes simultaneously. Hope arises because education is thought to offer improvement to individuals and society: it is sought as a remedy for personal and social ills. People think it will improve their life chances and so demand more of it, and electorates are persuaded that prosperity and social health depend upon it. This encourages politicians to give what they call priority to education: they take initiatives and spend our money on them. Then despair sets in. Individuals doubt whether the rewards of education are worth the tedium of pursuing it, and the populace baulks at the cost, asks tetchily about value for money and complains that education does not seem to have abolished poverty or urban crime. Neither Government nor the people can give up hope, so they seek to keep despair at bay by insisting that education be reformed. A period of febrile activity ensues, a phase that England is going through at present.

Apart from increasing already vast expenditures, the chief focus of effort is the teaching profession. Over entry to teaching, the qualifications required for this and the length, content and methods of teacher education central control has been made tighter and more detailed in-service training schemes proliferate, and advisory services burgeon. Teachers' contracts become more prescriptive, and salary increases are said to depend on performance. Teachers themselves are inspected, monitored, assessed and appraised to within an inch of their lives. To these direct measures are added other, indirect ones. The publication of inspectors' reports and league tables of schools' results are meant to act through 'naming and shaming'. Parents are encouraged to complain and to seek influence in the administration of schools. The creation of a national curriculum and the detailed prescription of 'hours' for literacy and numeracy is defended partly as a boost for standards in teaching.

After some twenty years of this it is beginning to dawn on politicians and public alike that this is a dead end. If money could have done the trick it would have done so by now. Education is opulent as never before. New expenditures produce only trivial and short-lived improvement. The attempt to make better teachers from above has produced a profession more demoralized than at any time in the last 100 years. The problems of education are more profound than either politicians or public imagine. The trouble with a formal education system is that it operates with groups, when it is only individuals who learn. Teachers know this and try to run their classes so as to accommodate individuals, but there are limits, within the system, to the extent to which they can do this. Officials tend to take the opposite course of standardizing what is offered, without understanding how far this inhibits learning.

Each child is unique. It is true that children's development follows the same sequence, but each child goes through the sequence at a different pace. Each child's capacities, deriving from the interaction of heredity and environment, are different. It is foolish to expect every child to do the same things at the same age, and barbaric to insist upon it. Standardized tests are at best irrelevant to a child's learning and at worst destructive.

There are many different theories about what happens when learning takes place, not all of them compatible with each other and with varying explanatory power. All of them agree, however, that learning takes place through the initiative and activity of the learner. Formal education systems rest on the opposite assumption, that learning takes place through the activity of the teacher, or worse of the Government. The idea of a curriculum devised by a committee, through which all children must proceed and be judged by their success or failure at it, is anti-educational.

Education is meant not just to develop individuals but also to prepare people for life in a society but it works best even for the latter purpose if those being educated are regarded as ends in themselves, not as little pitchers to be filled by gradgrinds with facts by the imperial pint, as circus animals trained to do trivial and demeaning tasks or as instruments of state or the economy.

A formal system which ignores all this will always produce at least as much despair as hope. There are no short cuts to improved achievement, though there are some to temporarily improved 'standards'. The national curriculum and performance-related pay are alike hopeless in the long run. Hope requires thought about children's development and learning and the redistribution of powers and duties in education so as to make both more fruitful. In particular it will mean restoring professional responsibility to teachers and the proper accountability that goes with it.

The formal system is so familiar and so pervasive that it is hard for people, even people in education, to see it plainly. The words used to describe it, even when they are not the purest jargon, usually obscure more than they reveal. This lexicon is addressed to learners of all ages and in all their varied circumstances, in the hope that it will goad them into thinking differently about what education might offer them. I know that it is easy to be cynical about a formal education system, but it is hard to be cynical enough.

Tyrrell Burgess
June 2002